Drew Provan

iPhone

covers iOS 7
4th edition updated for iPhone 5s and 5c

In easy steps is an imprint of In Easy Steps Limited
16 Hamilton Terrace · Holly Walk · Leamington Spa
Warwickshire · United Kingdom · CV32 4LY
www.ineasysteps.com

Fourth Edition

In Easy Steps Limited supports The Forest Stewardship Council (FSC),
the leading international forest certification organisation. All our titles
that are printed on Greenpeace approved FSC certified paper carry the
FSC logo.

MIX
Paper from
responsible sources
FSC® C020837

Printed and bound in the United Kingdom

ISBN 978-1-84078-608-8

Contents

7   Web Browsing   151

8   Email   165

9   **Accessibility Settings**   **177**

10   **Working with Apps**   **187**

11 Solving Problems   219

Index   233

1 The iPhone 5s and 5c

The latest iPhone comes in two models; the 5s and the 5c. They are both sophisticated and highly capable smartphones which are able to make calls, send texts and multimedia messages, browse the web, take and store video images and still photos, play games and keep you organized professionally and personally.

A Very Smart Smartphone!

Apple's first generation iPhone was launched in June 2007. Because of the advance publicity there was a feeding frenzy when launch day came, with customers queuing for many hours to get their hands on an iPhone.

There are several reasons for the excitement, including the Apple brand (stylish, functional and innovative). People already loved the iPod so a cell phone with iPod capabilities and a wide screen had major appeal. The sheer simplicity of operation, using a touchscreen rather than a plethora of buttons, had major appeal.

So this was a cell phone unlike any other. In addition to the usual telephony capabilities, this phone could play music, videos, YouTube and more. It could be used as a diary with easy synchronization to Microsoft Outlook or Apple Calendar. It would handle email (including Exchange Server) more easily. Its SMS app made messaging a breeze. Its browser made browsing the web easier than with previous smartphones.

In addition, there were applications such as Weather, Stocks, Maps and others. Despite criticisms from some quarters regarding the poor camera (2 megapixels in the first and second generation iPhones) and lack of video, along with the inability for the user to add more applications, the first generation iPhone was a huge success.

The second generation iPhone was launched in July 2008 and brought with it 3G, a much faster data network connection. In June 2009 the 3GS ("S" stands for "speed") was launched. The new iPhone 3GS brought with it the ability to capture video, Voice Control, which enables users to control the iPhone 3GS using voice commands, and numerous other features.

The 4G iPhone was launched in June 2010 and brought with it many refinements such as dual cameras, camera flash, FaceTime, Siri, higher resolution Retina Display screen and many other improvements over the previous models. The 4GS was launched in Summer 2011, and September 2012 saw the arrival of iPhone 5.

The iPhone 5s and 5c were launched in September 2013 which was a departure for Apple since it was the first time that they launched two models at the same time. The iPhone 5s is the more expensive model while the 5c is cheaper and comes in a range of bright colors.

The iPhone 5s and 5c both have similar storage options (they both come in 16GB and 32GB models and the 5s also has a 64GB option) and an 8 megapixel iSight camera. The iPhone 5s has a slightly faster processor and also a fingerprint identity sensor that can be used to lock your iPhone with a fingerprint.

The New icon pictured above indicates a new or enhanced feature introduced with the iPhone with iOS 7.

What Does It Do?

It would be easier to ask what it *doesn't* do! The iPhone, even as a basic cell phone, before you start adding applications, has many functions – probably enough for most people without actually having to add more apps of your own. But, since there are *thousands* of applications available for download, you can extend the functionality of the iPhone way beyond this. The iPhone is more like a small computer since you can store files, email, connect to other desktop computers, view documents including Word and PDF files, play games, look up recipes, manage your time, and many other functions.

Apps for work and play · Camera · On/Off button

Settings to customize your iPhone · App Store for more apps

11

Hot tip

Geotag is explained on page 42 and page 112.

Beware

You cannot remove the iPhone battery. This has to be carried out by Apple.

Don't forget

If you intend to keep videos as well as music on your iPhone it may be wise to opt for the higher capacity iPhone.

iPhone 5 Specifications

Cellular and wireless capabilities

The iPhone 5s and 5c are Quad band phones which use GSM and GPRS/EDGE.

There is also built-in Wi-Fi (802.11b/g) and Bluetooth. The iPhone also includes Global Positioning System (GPS) software, making it easy to geotag your pictures and videos. iPhone 5s and 5c also use 3G and 4G networks where available.

Battery

Unlike most cell phones, the user cannot take the battery out for replacement. The iPhone uses a built-in battery which is charged using a USB connection to the computer, or using the lightning charger supplied by Apple.

What do you get from a full charge?

- Talk time: Up to 10 hours on 3G

- Standby time: Up to 250 hours

- Internet use: Up to 8 hours on 3G, up to 10 hours Wi-Fi

- Video playback: Up to 10 hours

- Audio playback: Up to 40 hours

Internal storage

The iPhone uses internal flash drive storage. There is no SD or other card slot so the internal flash memory is all the storage you have – use it wisely!

iPhone 5s is available with 16GB, 32GB or 64GB storage capacity; the iPhone 5c is available with 16GB or 32GB storage.

In terms of color, you can get the iPhone 5s in Silver, Gold or Space Gray. The iPhone 5c comes in a wider range of colors: White, Pink, Yellow, Blue and Green.

What can I do with the storage space?

	16GB	32GB	64GB
Songs	3,500	7,000	14,000
Videos	20 hours	40 hours	80 hours
Photos	20,000	25,000	50,000

Sensors in the iPhone

There are four sensors in the iPhone: the Three-Axis Gyro, the Accelerometer, Proximity Sensor and the Ambient Light Sensor.

The *Accelerometer* enables the phone to detect rotation and position. This is important when switching from portrait to landscape viewing. The Accelerometer is also used in many of the iPhone game apps such as *Labyrinth* (below) which uses the Accelerometer to good effect – as you tilt the iPhone the ball bearing moves across a virtual board.

The *Proximity Sensor* switches off the iPhone screen when you make a call – it senses that the phone is close to the ear, saving valuable power. The *Ambient Light Sensor* adjusts the iPhone screen to the ambient lighting, again saving energy if a bright screen is not required.

The iPhone Itself

Unlike most cell phones, the iPhone is unusual since it has very few physical buttons.

Buttons you need to know on the iPhone

- Sleep/Wake (On/Off)
- Ring/Silent
- Volume controls
- Home button

On/Off/Sleep/Wake up, on the top of the body

Ring/Silent on the side

Volume controls on the side

Home button

Sleep/Wake

Press and briefly hold this button if your iPhone is switched off. You will see the Apple logo and the loading screen will start up. You will then be taken to the Home screen (opposite page). If you wish to put your phone away, press the Sleep/Wake button to put your phone to sleep.

Ring/Silent

You often want your phone on silent, during meetings for example. The Ring/Silent button can be toggled up and down. When you see the red line, this means the iPhone is on silent.

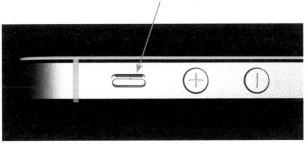

Pressing the Home button takes you back to the Home screen from any app you are using.

The Home button

This does what the name suggests and brings you back to the Homepage from wherever you are. If you are browsing applications in another screen, pressing the Home button will bring you right back to the Homepage. If you are using an app, pressing Home will close the app. If you are on a phone call, pressing the Home button lets you access your email or other apps.

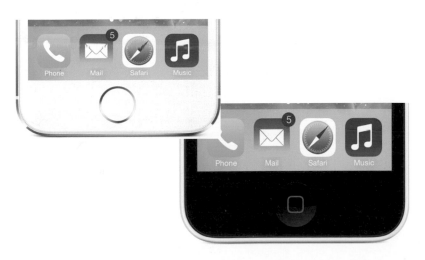

On the iPhone 5s the Home button can also be used as a fingerprint sensor for unlocking the phone with your unique fingerprint.

Other Buttons on the iPhone

Volume controls

Volume is controlled using two separate buttons – a **+** and **–** button (increase and decrease volume respectively). You can easily adjust the volume of the audio output when you are listening to the Music app, or when you are making a phone call. If you cannot hear the caller very well try increasing the volume.

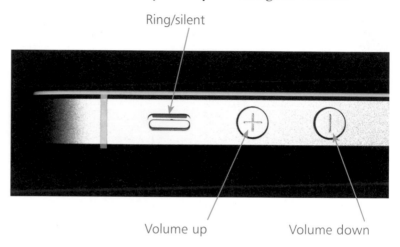

Ring/silent

Volume up   Volume down

The Nano SIM slot

The iPhone 5 uses a nano SIM (much smaller than micro SIM which is used in older iPhone models). Apple provides a SIM removal tool in the iPhone box.

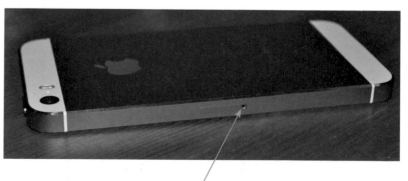

Insert the SIM tool into this hole and push it firmly. The SIM card holder will pop out and you can remove it and insert a SIM card

Lightning connector, speaker, microphone, and headset jack
These are located at the bottom of the iPhone.

Headset jack   Lightning connector

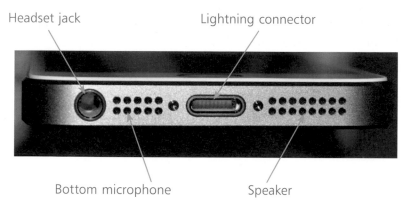

Bottom microphone   Speaker

Back view of the iPhone 5s
This shows the location of the main camera and the LED flash
(flash is not available for the front camera).

LED flash (and torch)

Rear microphone

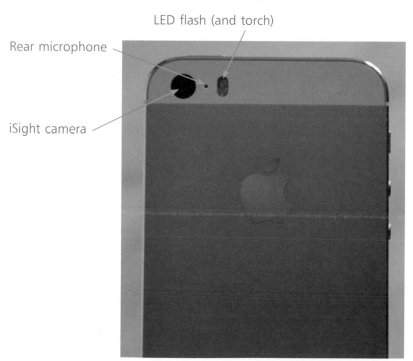

iSight camera

Setting up your iPhone

Before you can do anything on your iPhone you will need to activate it.

Once you switch on the new iPhone 5s or 5c (press the On/Off button) you will be taken through a series of screens where you set up various options.

Even though the initial setup is carried out wirelessly, you should plug your iPhone 5 into iTunes on your Mac or PC regularly to make sure you have a recent backup of the iPhone in case you lose or damage the iPhone.

Initially, there will be a series of setup screens to move through before you can use the iPhone: These include the following options (a lot of these can be skipped during the setup and accessed later from the **Settings** app).

- **Language.** Select the language you want to use

- **Country.** Select the country in which you are located

- **Wi-Fi network.** Select a Wi-Fi network to connect to the Internet. If you are at home, this will be your own Wi-Fi network, if available. If you are at a Wi-Fi hotspot then this will appear on your network list

- **Location Services.** This determines whether your iPhone can use your geographical location for apps that use this type of information (such as Maps)

- **Set Up iPhone.** You can use this to set up your iPhone from scratch, or restore it from a backup that has been created via iCloud or on iTunes

- **Apple ID.** You can register with this to be able to access a range of Apple facilities, such as iCloud, purchase items on iTunes or the App Store, Facetime, Messages and iBooks. You can also create an Apple ID whenever you first access one of the relevant apps

- **iCloud.** This is Apple's online service for sharing and backing up content. See pages 34-39 for details

- **Find My iPhone.** This is a service that can be activated so that you can locate your iPhone if it is lost or stolen. This is done via the online iCloud site at **www.icloud.com**

- **Touch ID.** This can be used on the iPhone 5s to create a fingerprint ID that can be used to unlock the phone

- **Create a Passcode.** This can be used on create a four digit code for unlocking the phone. This step can be skipped if required

- **Siri** This is the voice assistant that can be used to find things on your iPhone and on the Web

- **Diagnostic information.** This enables information about your iPhone to be sent to Apple

- **Get Started.** Once the setup process has been completed you can start using your iPhone

The Home Screen

What's on the Home screen?

When you turn the iPhone on you will see some icons which are fixed, such as the top bar with the time and battery charge indicator, as well as the Dock at the bottom which holds four apps. By default, your iPhone will have Phone, Mail, Safari and Music on the bottom Dock. You can move these off the Dock if you want, but Apple puts these here because they are the most commonly-used apps, and having them on the Dock makes them easy to find.

Just above the Dock you will see two dots. The dots represent each of your screens – the more apps you install, the more screens you will need to accommodate them (you are allowed 11 in all). The illustration here shows an iPhone with two screens, and the Home Screen is the one we are viewing. If you flicked to the next screen, the second dot would be white and the first one would be black. In effect, these are meant to let you know where you are at any time.

Hot tip

You can actually install more apps than the iPhone can show but you will need to do a Spotlight search (see page 44) for the app if you wish to use it.

Beware

The Battery indicator is fairly crude. For a more accurate guide, try switching on Battery % in Settings.

Signal strength, network and Wi-Fi   Bluetooth icon   Battery

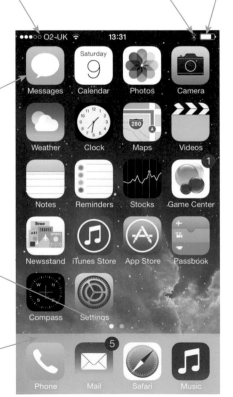

Default apps (which can be moved around but not deleted)

Dots representing the number of screens. Tap on a dot to move to that screen, or swipe left and right to move between screens

The Dock, where apps can be placed and appear on all screens

Default Applications

The iPhone comes with applications that are part of the operating system. The core set here cannot be deleted.

 Messages

 Notes

 Calendar

 Photos

 Calculator

 Clock

 Camera

 Settings

 Maps

 iTunes Store

 Phone

 Weather

 Stocks

 App Store

 Mail

 Voice Memos

 Safari

 Game Center

 Music

 Videos

 Newsstand

 Reminders

 Contacts

Don't forget

You cannot delete any of the standard apps – only the ones you add yourself.

Don't forget

Other useful apps, such as iBooks, Podcasts, Trailers, iPhoto, iMovie, GarageBand, Pages, Numbers and Keynote can be downloaded from the App Store.

The iPhone Dock

By default, there are four apps on the Dock at the bottom of the screen. These are the four that Apple thinks you will use most frequently:

- **Phone**, for calls

- **Mail**, for email

- **Safari**, for web browsing

- **Music**

You can rearrange the order in which the Dock apps appear:

1 Tap and hold on one of the Dock apps until it starts to jiggle

2 Drag the app into its new position

3 Click once on the **Home** button to return from edit mode

Hot tip

Just above the Dock is a line of small white dots. These indicate how many screens of content there are on the iPhone. Tap on one of the dots to go to that screen.

...cont'd

Adding and removing Dock apps

You can also remove apps from the Dock and add new ones:

1 To remove an app from the Dock tap and hold it and drag it onto the main screen area

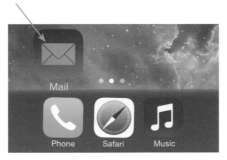

2 To add an app to the Dock tap and hold it and drag it onto the Dock

Don't forget

If items are removed from the Dock they are still available in the same way from the main screen.

23

3 The number of items that can be added to the Dock is restricted to a maximum of four as the icons do not resize

4 Click once on the **Home** button to return from edit mode

Software Version iOS 7

iOS 7 is the operating system for the iPhone and it brings in many new features. The whole interface has been redesigned to give it a more up-to-date and vibrant appearance and, although there are no new preinstalled apps, there have been a number of improvements in the existing ones to ensure that iOS 7 is the most advanced mobile operating system out there.

A quick round-up of the features of iOS 7 is shown below:

New design

iOS 7 is one of the most dramatic cosmetic changes to the operating system in its history. It was overseen by the designer Jonathan Ive, who was responsible for some of the most iconic Apple devices including the iMac, iPod and iPhone. The design is intended to be a cleaner, simpler one for the icons and apps and moves away from previous styles, which relied on the interpretation of everyday materials such as paper, leather, wood and felt.

Control Center

This is a way of quickly accessing some of the commonly used functions on the iPhone. It can be activated by swiping up from the bottom of any screen.

The interpretation of everyday items in the design of computer interfaces is known as skeuomorphic.

Multitasking

Some previous versions of iOS had a multitasking bar, but this has been redesigned in iOS 7 so that it provides a full screen option for viewing and using your open apps and also closing the ones that you do not want to currently use.

Camera and Photos

This includes options for taking photos in different ratios, a new way of organizing and viewing your photos in the Photos app and special effects added to the editing functions.

Siri improvements

The voice assistant function that was introduced in iOS 6 has been improved further with a new interface and a wider range of content over which it can search.

Safari improvements

The iOS 7 web browser now has a unified Search/Address bar, an improved tabs view and shared links so that you can view your social networking updates through Safari.

App Store improvements

The iPhone App Store has been redesigned and includes a new feature that can show apps that are particularly relevant to your current location.

iOS 7 also has improvements to the Find My iPhone (or iPad) service and a range of options for business users, including improved security for personal data.

Beware

The touch screen works best using skin contact. You can buy special gloves that will work but standard gloves cannot be used.

The Touch Screen Display

The iPhone uses a touch-sensitive screen for input, using gestures and a virtual keyboard. The screen is 4 inches (diagonal) and has a resolution of 1136 x 640-pixel resolution at 326 PPI (Pixels Per Inch) – Apple has called this the *Retina Display* because the resolution is so high. This results in great clarity when viewing the browser or watching movies on the iPhone. Although the iPhone has a fingerprint-resistant coating it still gets grubby. A number of companies make screen protectors (sticky plastic sheets that cover the entire screen) but they are probably not necessary since the screen is made from scratch-resistant glass. You can also protect the other parts of the iPhone from scratching by using a protective case.

Touch screen features

The screen is able to detect touch using skin. If you wear gloves or try to tap the screen using a stylus nothing will happen – it responds best to skin.

Tapping

Tapping with one finger is used for lots of apps. It's a bit like clicking with the mouse. You tap apps to open them, to open hyperlinks, to select photo albums which then open, to enter text using the keyboard, and many other tasks.

Sliding

Sliding is another common action. When you first press the iPhone Home button you will see an option at the bottom of the screen to Slide to Unlock. Putting your finger on the arrow button then sliding all the way to the right will then take you to the Home Screen. You also use the slide action to answer phone calls and shut down the iPhone.

Dragging

This is used to move documents that occupy more than a screen's worth across the screen. Maps use this feature, as do web pages. Place your finger on the screen, keep it there and move the image to where you want it.

Pinching and spreading

If you are looking at a photo or text which you want to enlarge, you can spread two fingers apart and the image will become larger. Keep doing this until it's the size you want. If you want to zoom out and make the image smaller, pinch your fingers together.

Flicking

If you are faced with a long list, e.g. in Contacts, you can flick the list up or down by placing your finger at the bottom or top of the screen, keeping your finger on the screen, then flicking your finger downwards or upwards and the list will fly up or down.

Shake the iPhone

When entering text or copying and pasting, to undo what you have done, shake the iPhone. Shake again to redo.

Portrait or landscape mode

The iPhone is generally viewed in a portrait mode but for many tasks it is easier to turn the iPhone and work in landscape mode. If you're in Mail, or using Safari, the text will be larger. More importantly, the keys of the virtual keyboard will become larger making it easier to type accurately.

Entering text

The iPhone has predictive text, but this is unlike any you may have used before. The accuracy is astonishing. As you type, the iPhone will make suggestions before you complete a word. If you agree with the suggested word, tap the spacebar. If you disagree, tap the small "x" next to the word.

You can shake your iPhone to skip audio tracks, undo and redo text, and more.

To accept a spelling suggestion tap the spacebar. Reject the suggestion by clicking the "x". Over time your iPhone will learn new words.

27

Accept the capitalized word by tapping the spacebar

Accept the apostrophe by tapping the spacebar

Tapping the spacebar with two fingers at the same time also inserts a period.

Multitasking Window

The iPhone can run several programs at once and these can be managed by the Multitasking window. This has been redesigned for iOS 7 and it performs a number of tasks:

- It shows open apps

- It enables you to move between open apps and open different ones

- It enables apps to be closed (see next page)

Accessing Multitasking

The Multitasking option can be accessed from any screen on your iPhone, as follows:

1 Double-click on the **Home** button

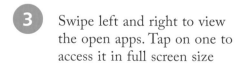

2 The currently-open apps are displayed, with their icon underneath them (except the Home screen). The most recently-used apps are shown first

3 Swipe left and right to view the open apps. Tap on one to access it in full screen size

Closing Items

The iPhone deals with open apps very efficiently. They do not interact with other apps, which increases security and also means that they can be open in the background, without using up a significant amount of processing power, in a state of semi-hibernation until they are needed. Because of this it is not essential to close apps when you move to something else. However, you may want to close apps if you feel you have too many open or if one stops working. To do this:

1 Access the Multitasking window. The currently-open apps are displayed

2 Press and hold on an app and swipe it to the top of the screen to close it. This does not remove it from the iPhone and it can be opened again in the usual way

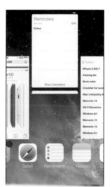

When you switch from one app to another, the first one stays open in the background. You can go back to it by accessing it from the Multitasking window or the Home screen.

3 The app is removed from its position in the Multitasking window

In the Control Center

The Control Center is a panel containing some of the most commonly used options within the **Settings** app. It can be accessed with one swipe and is an excellent function for when you do not want to have to go into Settings.

Accessing the Control Center

The Control Center can be accessed from any screen within iOS 7 and it can also be accessed from the Lock Screen:

The Control Center cannot be disabled from being accessed from the Home screen.

30

1 Tap on the **Settings** app

2 Tap on the **Control Center** tab and drag the **Access on Lock Screen** and **Access Within Apps** buttons On or Off to specify if the Control Center can be accessed from here (if both are Off, it can still be accessed from any Home screen)

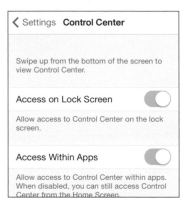

3 Swipe up from the bottom of any screen to access the Control Center panel

4 Tap on this button to hide the Control Center panel, or tap anywhere on the screen

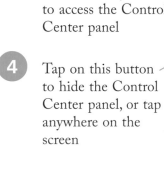

Control Center controls

The items that can be used in the Control Center are:

1 Use these controls for any music or video that is playing. Use the buttons to Pause/Play a track, go to the beginning or end and adjust the volume

2 Tap on this button to turn **Airplane mode** On or Off

3 Tap on this button to turn **Wi-Fi** On or Off

4 Tap on this button to turn **Bluetooth** On or Off

5 Tap on this button to turn **Do Not Disturb** mode On or Off

6 Tap on this button to access a **Clock**, including a stopwatch

7 Tap on this button to open the **Camera** app

8 Tap on this button to **Lock** or **Unlock** screen rotation. If it is locked, the screen will not change when you change the orientation of your iPhone

9 Tap on this button to activate the iPhone's **Torch**

Hot tip

The Torch function is very effective, particularly over short distances.

The Virtual Keyboard

The keys are small but when you touch them they become larger, which increases accuracy. The letter "T" below has been pressed and has become much larger.

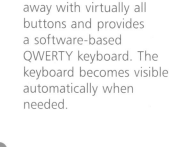

There are all the usual features of a computer keyboard, including spacebar, delete key , shift , numbers and symbols .

To correct a word, touch the word you want to correct and hold your finger on the word. You will see a magnifying glass. Move your finger to where you want the insertion point (|) to be, stop there and delete any wrong letters.

The keyboard has automatic spellcheck and correction of misspelled words. It has a dynamic dictionary (learns new words). Some keys have multiple options if you hold them down, e.g. hold down the £ key and you'll see the other characters.

Where's Caps Lock?

It is frustrating hitting the Caps key for every letter if you want to type a complete word in upper case. But you can activate Caps Lock easily:

- Go to **Settings > General**

- Select **Keyboard**

- Make sure the **Caps Lock** slider is set to **ON**

- While you are there, make sure the other settings are on, for example "**.**" **Shortcut** – this helps you add a period by tapping the spacebar twice

It's a good idea to activate Caps Lock. To use, just tap Shift twice – the shift button should turn blue if you have activated it properly in the Settings control panel.

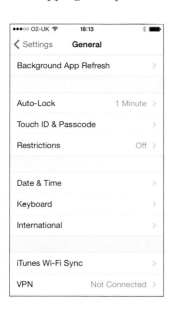

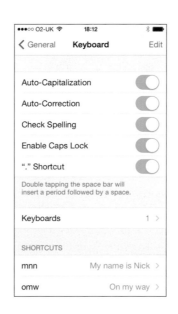

Other settings for the keyboard

- **Auto-Correction** suggests the correct word. If it annoys you, switch it off

- **Auto-Capitalization** is great for putting capitals in names

- Whilst the "**.**" **Shortcut** types a period every time you hit the spacebar twice and saves time when typing long emails, if you prefer not to use this, you can switch it off. Here's another neat trick – you can also insert a period by tapping the spacebar with two fingers simultaneously

iCloud and an Apple ID

Apple iCloud

This is a service that allows you to use the cloud to sync your data (calendars, contacts, mail, Safari bookmarks, and notes) wirelessly.

Once you are registered and set up, any entries or deletions to calendars and other apps are reflected in all devices using iCloud.

An Apple ID is required for using iCloud, and this can be obtained online at **https://appleid.apple.com/** or you can create an Apple ID when you first access an app on your iPhone that requires this for use. It is free to create an Apple ID and requires a username and password. Once you have created an Apple ID you can then use the full range of iCloud service.

Start using iCloud on the iPhone and computers

Don't forget

The iPhone apps that require an Apple ID to access their full functionality include: iTunes Store, iMessages, iBooks, FaceTime, Game Center and the App Store.

1 Open the iCloud System Preferences (Mac) or Control Panel (PC)

2 Log into your iCloud account with your Apple ID (you only need to do this once – it will remember your details)

3 Check **On** the items that you want synced by iCloud

Don't forget

Using iCloud removes the need to sync items such as contacts, calendars, notes and photos on other iCloud-enabled devices that you have, such as tablets and computers: iCloud does it all automatically.

4 On your iPhone, open the **Settings > iCloud** and select the items you want to be used by iCloud. All of the selected items will be reflected on the equivalent apps on your computer

Using iCloud online

Once you have created an Apple ID you will automatically have an iCloud account. This can be used to sync your data from your iPhone and you can also access your content online from the iCloud website at **www.icloud.com**

1 Enter your Apple ID details

2 Click on the **iCloud** button from any section to go to other areas

3 The full range of iCloud apps is displayed, including those for Pages, Numbers and Keynote

Hot tip

iCloud lets you sync emails, contacts, calendars and other items wirelessly (no need to physically plug the iPhone into the computer).

Syncing Your Data

Your iPhone can store several types of information:

- Calendar
- Email
- Contacts
- Music
- Photos
- Videos
- Podcasts
- Apps (applications, i.e. programs)
- Documents

With iCloud, items such as Calendars, Contacts and Reminders get synced automatically once it has been set up. With iTunes on a computer you can sync items such as Music, Movies, TV Shows, Podcasts and iBooks. You will need to choose which media files and apps get synced when you plug your iPhone into your computer. You can also select to have iTunes sync your content automatically or do it manually for more control:

- You can opt *not* to open iTunes automatically when you plug the iPhone in

- You can also choose to sync some types of content *manually* rather than automatically. To do this, scroll down to the bottom of the Summary window, when your iPhone is connected to iTunes on a computer, and check on the **Manually manage music and videos** button

When you connect your iPad to your computer it will show up under the **Devices** heading in the iTunes sidebar.

To sync your data with iTunes on a Mac or Windows PC:

1 Connect your iPhone to the computer with the lightning USB connector. Tap on the **Set up as new iPhone** button and tap on **Continue**

2 Tap on the **Get Started** button

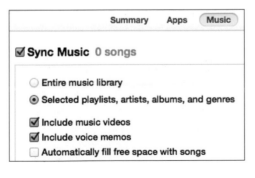

3 Select a category to sync from the top toolbar, e.g. Music, Movies or TV Shows and select the options for how you want the items synced

4 Tap on the **Apply** button to sync the selected items to your iPhone

Apply

Hot tip

Automated syncs take the guesswork out of syncing.

Backup and Restore

Like any electronic device it is important to back up the content on your iPhone. This means that if something goes wrong with it then you will be able to restore the content from the backup. This can be done through iTunes on either a Mac or Windows PC. The backup can be also be sent to iCloud so that your content is stored there.

To back up your iPhone

The backup process can be performed using iTunes on either a Mac or Windows PC:

Hot tip

If you select to back up your iPhone to iCloud, this will be done automatically on a regular basis.

1 Connect your iPhone to the computer with the lightning USB connector and click on it in the left-hand iTunes panel, under **Devices**

> **DEVICES**
> 📱 Nick's iPhone 🔋 ⏏

2 In the Summary window, select how you would like the backup to be performed, i.e. with iCloud or on the computer to which your iPhone is connected

> **Backups**
>
> **Automatically Back Up**
> ⦿ iCloud
>   Back up the most important data on your iPhone to iCloud.
> ○ This computer
>   A full backup of your iPhone will be stored on this computer.
>   ☐ Encrypt iPhone backup
>   This will also back up account passwords used on this iPhone.
>   [Change Password...]

3 Tap on the **Back Up Now** button

> **Manually Back Up and Restore**
> Manually back up your iPhone to this computer or restore a backup stored on this computer.
>
> [Back Up Now]   [Restore Backup...]
>
> **Latest Backups:**
> Your iPhone has never been backed up to iCloud.
> 11/11/2013 15:45 to this computer

4 The progress of the backup is displayed at the top of the iTunes window

> Backing up "Nick's iPhone"...
> ▓▓▓▓▓▓▓▓▓▓▓▓▓▓▓▓▓▓ ⊗

To restore the iPhone from a backup

If something does go wrong with your iPhone you can restore it to the latest backed up version. To do this:

1 Connect your iPhone to the computer with the lightning USB connector and click on it in the left-hand iTunes panel, under **Devices**

DEVICES

📱 Nick's iPhone

2 In the Summary window, click on the **Restore Backup** button

Restore Backup...

3 If you have made more than one backup you will be able to select which one you want to restore your iPhone with (the most recent one is usually the best option). Tap on the **Restore** button

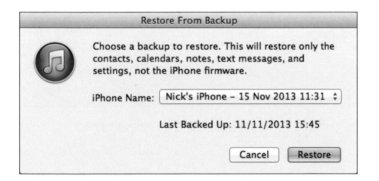

Restore From Backup

Choose a backup to restore. This will restore only the contacts, calendars, notes, text messages, and settings, not the iPhone firmware.

iPhone Name: Nick's iPhone – 15 Nov 2013 11:31 ⬍

Last Backed Up: 11/11/2013 15:45

Cancel   Restore

4 The progress of the restore process is shown by this window and a similar message will display on your iPhone's screen

iPhone

Restoring iPhone from backup...

Time remaining: Less than a minute

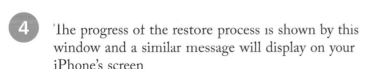

Hot tip

Unlike an iPod, where you have to eject it from the PC or Mac before unplugging, you don't have to eject the iPhone – simply unplug it.

Headphones

Apple supplies headphones that look a bit like iPod headphones. But there is a major difference: the iPhone headphones have a control on the right earpiece cable. This control houses the microphone needed for phone conversations when the headphones are plugged in. The control also allows the audio volume to be adjusted to make it louder or quieter.

By clicking the control, audio will pause. Two clicks in quick succession will skip to the next track.

Hot tip

The iPhone headphones are highly sophisticated and can be used to make calls, and divert callers to voicemail.

Press here ONCE to pause audio or answer call (press again at end of call)

To decline call press and hold for ~2 seconds

To switch to incoming or on-hold call, press once

Press here TWICE to skip to next track

To use Voice Control, press and hold

(this tiny control unit also contains the microphone!)

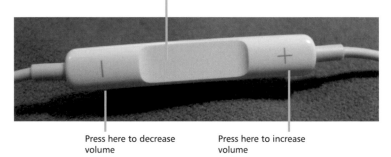

Press here to decrease volume

Press here to increase volume

Uses for the headphones – this is pretty obvious but consider

- Listening to music, podcasts, audio books
- Listening to the radio
- Watching movies
- Making phone calls
- Dictating VoiceMemos
- Giving Voice commands to your iPhone

Audio and Video Playback

As you would expect, the iPhone supports a number of audio and video formats. The iPhone supports audio in the form of AAC, Protected AAC, MP3, MP3 VBF, Audible (formats 2, 3, and 4), Apple Lossless, AIFF and WAV. In terms of video, the iPhone supports H.264 video up to 1080p, 60 frames per second, High Profile level 4.2 with AAC-LC audio up to 160 Kbps, 48kHz, stereo audio in .m4v, .mp4, and .mov file formats; MPEG-4 video up to 2.5 Mbps, 640 by 480 pixels, 30 frames per second, Simple Profile with AAC-LC audio up to 160 Kbps per channel, 48kHz, stereo audio in .m4v, .mp4, and .mov file formats; Motion JPEG (M-JPEG) up to 35 Mbps, 1280 by 720 pixels, 30 frames per second, audio in ulaw, PCM stereo audio in .avi file format.

Audio files are played using the Music app in portrait or landscape mode, as does video content.

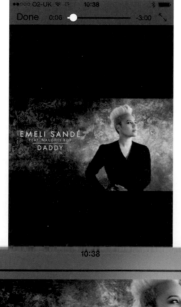

Camera

The iPhone 5s and 5c have a main, iSight, camera (back of phone) and a second camera on the front. The main camera is 8 megapixels (MP), and can shoot high resolution stills and HD video. The main camera also has a flash. The front VGA camera is used for FaceTime calls, and can takes photos and videos at 1.2 MP (photos) and HD video (720p) up to 30 frames per second.

Both photos and videos can be geotagged, so you can see where in the world you were when the photo or video was shot.

Geotagging helps you determine where the photo was taken but you need to switch on **Settings > Privacy > Location Services**.

1 Swipe left and right here to move between standard photo mode, square mode, panorama, video and slow-mo

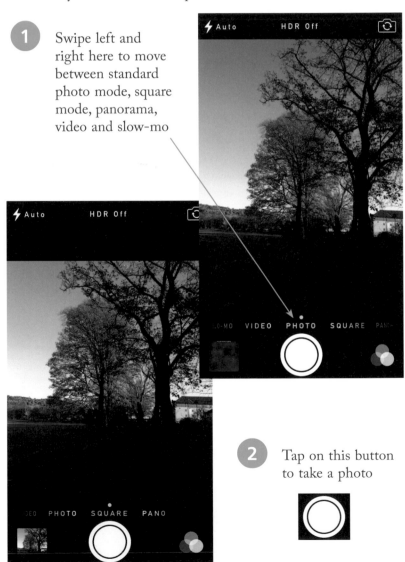

2 Tap on this button to take a photo

3 Tap on this button to toggle between the front- and back-facing cameras

4 Tap on this button to select a filter effect to add to the photo you are going to take

Shooting video

Select the Video option as shown in Step 1 and you will see a Record button (red circle). Press to record video then press again to stop recording.

Searching with Spotlight

If you want to find things on your iPhone, there is a built-in search engine, Spotlight. This can search over numerous items on your iPhone and these can be selected within Settings:

Spotlight settings

Within the Settings app you can select which items the Spotlight search operates over. To do this:

1   Tap on the **Settings** app

Don't forget

To return to the Home screen from the Search page, tap once anywhere on the screen.

2   Tap on **General** tab

3   Tap on the **Spotlight Search** link

4   Tap on an item to exclude it from the Spotlight search. Items with a tick will be included

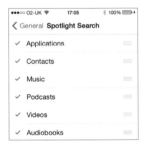

Hot tip

Enter the name of an app into the Spotlight search box and tap on the result to launch the app from here.

Accessing Spotlight

The Spotlight search box can be accessed from any screen by pressing and swiping downwards on any free area of the Home screen. This also activates the keyboard.

Searching with Siri

Siri is the iPhone voice assistant that provides answers to a variety of questions by looking at your iPhone and also web services. Initially, Siri can be set up within the **Settings** app:

1 In the **General** section, tap on the **Siri** link

2 Drag the **Siri** button to **On** to activate the Siri functionality. Tap on the links to select a language, set voice feedback and allow access to your details

Questioning Siri

Once you have set up Siri, you can start putting it to work with your queries. To do this:

1 Hold down the **Home** button until the Siri window appears

2 Ask a question such as, **Show me my calendar**

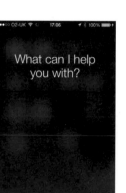

3 The results are displayed by Siri. Tap on an item to view its details. Tap on the microphone button to ask another question of Siri

You can ask Siri questions relating to the apps on your iPhone and also general questions, such as weather conditions around the world, or sports results. The results will be displayed by Siri or, if it does not know the answer, a web or Wikipedia link will be displayed instead.

Customizing the iPhone

Applications

The iPhone comes with many apps preinstalled by Apple. These can be moved around, or even placed on a different screen, but you cannot delete them from the iPhone. These apps are the core features of the iPhone.

The App Store has thousands of apps which we will look at later. Many are free while others are available for purchase. With so many apps available for download the chances are that there will be an app for most things you might want to do.

Ringtones

Apple has supplied several but people will always want to have their own unique ringtone. You can buy these from the App Store or make your own using iTunes or GarageBand. You can assign a specific ringtone to someone in your Contacts list so you know it's them calling when the phone rings.

Backgrounds and wallpapers

Again, there are several to choose from but you can make your own (usc onc of your photos) or you can download from third party suppliers. Try browsing the Internet for wallpapers or use a specific app.

Don't forget

GarageBand is Apple's music-making app and it can be downloaded from the App Store.

Accessorizing the iPhone

You can use a screen protector to prevent scratches on the screen. There are many iPhone cases available. These are mainly plastic but leather cases are available as well. Placing your iPhone in a case or cover helps prevent marks or scratches on the phone.

Headphones

If you want to use headphones other than those provided by Apple, that's fine. You may get better sound from your music but you will not have the inbuilt microphone, which is very useful when you make a phone call.

Lightning to 30-pin Adapter

Most of us have chargers round the house, or radio alarms and other iPhone/iPod music players that use the standard 30-pin dock connector. Apple has replaced this connector with the Lightning Connector which will make all your other 30-pin dock connector devices obsolete unless you buy the Apple Lightning to 30-pin Adapter. This should give a new lease of life to your existing devices that use the older 30-pin dock.

Bluetooth drains power on your iPhone. Try to switch it off if you don't need it.

USB to Lightning charger cable

With extensive use the iPhone battery may not last the whole day so you will probably need to carry around a spare charging cable. The USB to Lightning cable means you can plug it in to your PC or Mac at work and charge your iPhone during the day.

User Settings

There are many settings you can adjust in order to set the iPhone up to work the way you want. These will be discussed in detail later but they are shown briefly here.

As well as the settings already on the iPhone, many apps will have panels for their settings. If an app is not working the way you want, have a look under the Settings Control Panel and scroll to the bottom to see if your app has installed a settings panel.

Don't forget

The Wi-Fi Settings are grouped together with those for **Airplane Mode**, **Bluetooth**, **Mobile** and **Carrier**. Bluetooth can be used to scan for other compatible devices, which then have to be paired with the iPhone so that they can share content wirelessly.

Wi-Fi

Keep this off if you want to conserve power. Switching it on will let you join wireless networks if they are open or if you have the password.

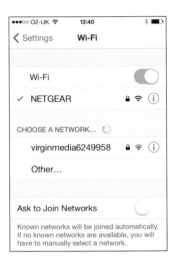

Don't forget

If a Settings option has an On/Off button next to it, this can be changed by swiping the button to either the left or right. Green indicates that the option is **On**.

Notification Center

This is where you can set what items appear in the Notification Center, which is accessed by swiping down from the top of the screen.

Control Center

This is a set of shortcuts for regularly used items. See pages 28-29 for details.

Do Not Disturb

Use this to specify times when you do not receive alerts or FaceTime video calls.

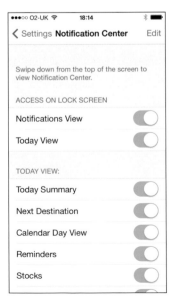

General

This contains the largest range of settings, that can be used to check the software version on your iPhone, search settings, accessibility, Touch ID, date and time, keyboard settings and resetting your iPhone.

Many apps have their own settings. Go to **Settings** on the iPhone and scroll down to the bottom of the screen.

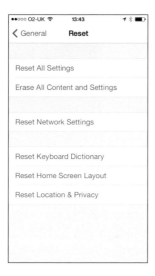

Sounds

You can place the phone on vibrate or have the ringtone on. You can assign different tones for different contacts.

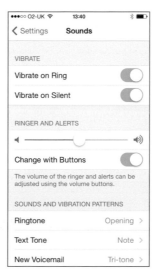

You can assign specific ringtones to selected contacts.

...cont'd

Wallpapers & Brightness

Wallpaper is what you see when you press the Home Button when the iPhone is locked. Use your own images or download from third party suppliers. The iPhone will adjust brightness automatically. If you always prefer it dimmer or brighter – switch automatic brightness off.

Your data on the iPhone is easily accessible if your iPhone is stolen. Use Passcode Lock and turn **Erase Data** On to wipe phone after 10 failed attempts.

50

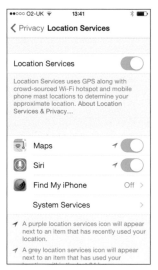

Privacy

This contains a number of privacy options, including activating **Location Services**, so that apps such as Maps and Siri can use your location, using GPS. Location Services also has to be turned On if you want to use the **Find My iPhone** feature.

One of the iCloud functions is the iCloud Keychain **(Settings > iCloud > Keychain)**. If this is enabled, it can keep all of your passwords and credit card information up-to-date across multiple devices and remember them when you use them on websites. The information is encrypted and controlled through your Apple ID.

iCloud

This is where you can specify the items that are shared with the online iCloud service. This includes On/Off options for apps such as Notes and Calendars and additional options for the Photos app.

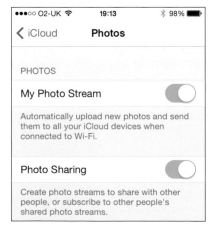

Mail, Contacts, Calendars

Use this for setting up new email accounts and also specifying settings for your existing accounts.

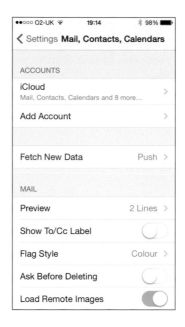

Apps' Settings

A lot of apps have their own settings, including the pre-installed ones. Tap on an app's name in the Settings app to view its own specific settings. It is worth checking Settings after you install an app to see if it has installed a settings file, since it may contain useful features to help you set it up exactly the way you want.

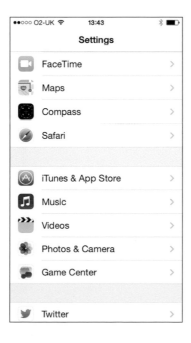

Using the Lock Screen

To save power it is possible to set your iPhone screen to auto-lock. This is the equivalent of the sleep option on a traditional computer. To do this:

1 Tap on the **Settings** app

2 Tap on the **General** tab

General

3 Tap on the **Auto-Lock** link

Auto-Lock   1 Minute >

4 Tap on the time of non-use after which you wish the screen to be locked

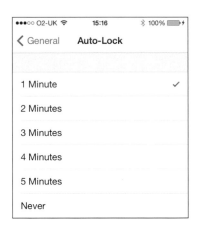

●●●○○ O2-UK 🛜   15:16   ✻ 100% 🔋⚡

‹ General   Auto-Lock

1 Minute   ✓

2 Minutes

3 Minutes

4 Minutes

5 Minutes

Never

5 Once the screen is locked, swipe here to the right to unlock the screen

Touch ID

Fingerprint sensor

The iPhone 5s has a fingerprint sensor that can be used to unlock your iPhone. This is done by pressing your thumb or finger on the sensor to create a unique fingerprint code. To set this up:

1 Select **Settings > General** and tap on the **Touch ID & Passcode** link

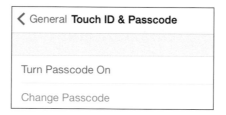

2 A passcode is required before Touch ID can be activated. Tap on the **Turn Passcode On** link

3 Enter a four-digit passcode

4 Tap on the **Touch ID** link

5 Tap on the **Add a Fingerprint** link. This presents a screen for creating your Touch ID. Place your finger on the Home button several times until the Touch ID is created. Use this to unlock your iPhone at the Lock Screen

The fingerprint sensor is very effective, although it may take a bit of practise until you can get the right position for your finger to unlock the iPhone, first time, everytime.

Data Roaming

Most of us travel abroad for business or pleasure. We like to take our cell phones to keep in touch with friends, family and the office. Call charges are much higher from overseas, and if you want to receive data (email, browse the web, and other activities) you will need to switch on Data Roaming.

Switch on Data Roaming

 Go to **Settings > General > Mobile**

 Switch **Data Roaming** On if required

3 Switch Off when not needed

But beware – the cost of receiving data is very high and will be added to your phone bill. Your data package with your network supplier (e.g. AT&T, O2 etc.) will not cover the cost of downloading data using foreign networks!

Beware

Data Roaming allows you to receive data when away from your home country, but is very expensive.

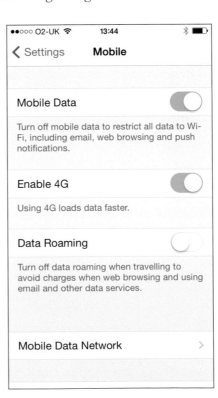

2 The Phone Functions

In this chapter we will look at how to use the phone functions to make and receive calls, maintain contact lists and make video calls using FaceTime.

Assigning Ringtones

The iPhone has a number of polyphonic ringtones built in, or you can buy more from iTunes or even make your own. You can have the default tone for every caller or you can assign a specific tone for a contact.

To assign a ringtone

1 Tap on the **Phone** app

2 Select a contact then click **Edit**

3 Click on the **Ringtone** link

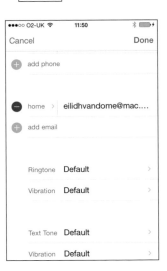

4 Choose the ringtone you wish to assign and tap on the **Done** button

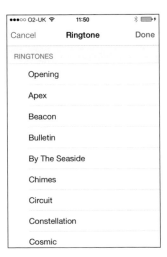

Making Calls Using Keypad

Although you can do a multitude of things with the iPhone, one of its basic functions is making phone calls. To do this:

1 Tap on the **Phone** app

2 Select the keypad icon. This brings up a standard keypad on the touchscreen

3 Dial the number. This appears at the top of the screen as you add it

Make FaceTime Video Calls

To use FaceTime

- The caller and recipient must both use iPhone 4 or later

- Alternatively, you can use a FaceTime-enabled Mac

- FaceTime calls can be made using Wi-Fi or Cellular

The FaceTime settings

1 Go to **Settings > FaceTime > On**

2 Select contact you wish to call

3 Tap **FaceTime**

4 Make FaceTime call

5 Recipient must tap **Accept**

If you have already had a FaceTime video call with someone you can go to **Recents** and make another FaceTime call.

Actions during a FaceTime call

1 Tap on this button to mute the call. You will still be able to see the caller

2 Tap on this button to toggle between the front and back cameras

3 Tap on this button to end a FaceTime call

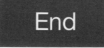

Using the Contacts List

The Contacts app acts like your own address book on the iPhone:

1 Tap the **Contacts** app on the Home Screen

2 Flick up or down until you find the contact you wish to call

3 Select the action you wish to take, e.g. send text message, phone the contact

Add photo to contact

If you want to assign a photo to a contact, access the contact, tap **Edit** and tap **Edit** again next to their name. Select a photo or take a new one. This gives a more personalized phone call, instead of just seeing a name or a number on the screen.

Using the Favorites List

People you call regularly can be added to your favorites list. This is the first icon (from the left) when you open the phone application.

To add someone to your favorites list

1 Open **Contacts**

2 Select the contact you wish to add

3 Tap **Add to Favorites**

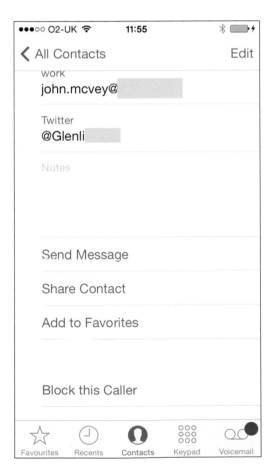

Add the contacts you call most to your Favorites List.

You can rearrange the Favorites list order by tapping Edit then moving your contacts up or down until you have them in the order you want.

Recents List

Recent calls you have made or missed are listed under Recents.

Missed calls

● These are in the **Missed** tab and are listed in red

● **All** shows the calls made, received and missed

● Calls made are shown by the icon

● Calls received are shown without an icon

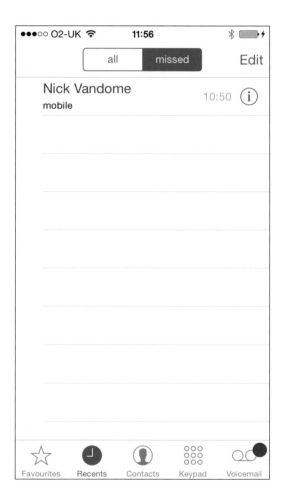

To return a call using Recents list
From the names shown in the Recents list, simply tap the name of the person you wish to call.

Answering Calls

When you receive a call the iPhone will either ring or vibrate, depending on your iPhone settings. If the iPhone is locked, you will see the name of the caller on the screen and you will need to tap on the **Answer** button. If the iPhone is unlocked when the call comes in, you will be given the option to **Answer** or **Decline** (and send to voicemail).

When you receive an incoming call, you can answer by tapping on the green **Answer** button.

If you do not want to take the call and let it go to voicemail, tap on **Decline** or tap on the the **Remind Me** button to be sent a reminder about the missed call at a certain time.

Tap on the **Message** button to send a text message to the person phoning.

After answering a call you will see the various options available.

Do Not Disturb

There are times when you do not want to see or hear Notifications from apps, or receive phone calls. For example, during the night you may want to divert all calls to voicemail rather than be woken up by phone calls.

1 Open **Settings > Do Not Disturb**

2 Slide the slider to **On** if you want to switch on Do Not Disturb

Allow some callers to get through

You may want to allow friends and family, or those in your favorites list to get through and not be diverted to voicemail.

1 Open **Settings > Do Not Disturb**

2 Choose the scheduled time (if you wish to schedule)

3 **Allow Calls From** > choose **Everyone, No One, Favorites**, or specific groups

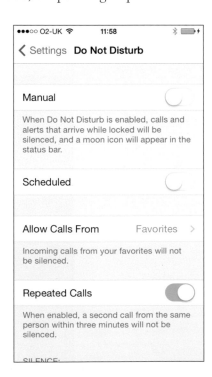

Missed Calls

It happens to all of us from time to time: the boss calls and somehow you managed to miss it. If your iPhone was locked when he called, you can see at a glance that he has called.

You can find out exactly when he called by looking at the missed calls list.

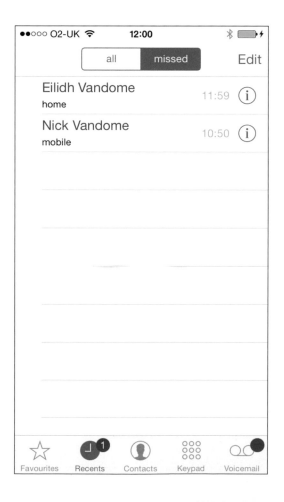

Make the Most of Contacts

The Contacts application on the iPhone lets you call someone, send them an SMS or MMS, email them, and assign them specific ringtones.

Add someone to Contacts

If you get a call from someone who is not in your contacts list, you can add them from the Phone app.

1 Open the Phone app and tap on the **Recents** button on the bottom toolbar

2 Recent calls and their numbers will be displayed

3 Select a number and tap on the **Create New Contact** button

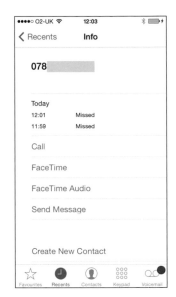

4 Enter the details for the contact and tap on the **Done** button. The contact's details will be added to the Contacts app

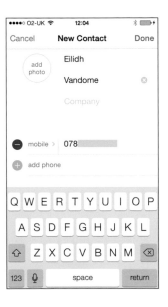

Adding Contacts

You can also add contacts directly into the Contacts app, so you can then access their details. To do this:

1 Tap on the Contacts app

2 Tap on the **+** button to add details for a new contact

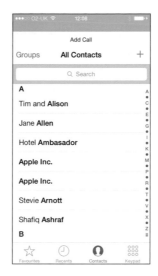

3 Enter the details for the contact, including First and Last Name, Phone, Email and Address. Tap on the **Add Photo** button to browse to a photo, or take one with the camera. Tap on the green **+** buttons to include extra items for each field

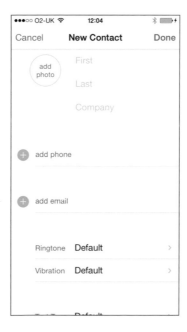

4 Tap on the **Done** button. The contact's details will be added to the Contacts app

Deleting Contacts

It is relatively easy to delete contacts:

1 **Tap** the contact you wish to remove

2 Once their details are loaded tap **Edit** at the top right

You contacts can also be accessed and managed through your iCloud online account, if you have set one up, using an Apple ID.

68

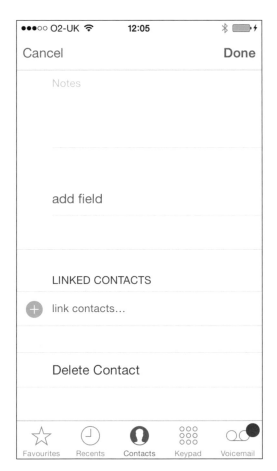

3 Scroll down to the bottom of the screen and tap **Delete Contact**

4 That's it!

Make Calls Using Headphones

You don't have to hold the iPhone to your ear each time you want to make a call. It is often more convenient to use the headphones. This means you can keep the phone on the desk and make notes during the call.

The headphones are very sophisticated – the right cord contains a white rectangular button which is useful when listening to music – but they are also great for making calls.

How to use the headphones

Make a phone call	Dial as normal and speak normally. You will hear the caller via the headphones and they will hear your voice, which is picked up by the inbuilt microphone
Answer a call	Click the middle of the control button once
Decline a call	Press the middle of the controller and hold for ~two seconds (you will hear two low beeps to confirm)
End call	Press the middle of the controller once
If already on a call and you wish to switch to an incoming call and put current call on hold	Press the middle button once to talk to Caller 2 (and press again to bring Caller 1 back)
Switch to incoming call and end the current call	Press and hold the middle of the controller for ~two seconds (you will hear two low beeps to confirm)
Use Voice Control to dial the number	Press and hold the middle button

Beware

You can use third party headphones with the iPhone but it is likely you will lose some functionality.

Hide or Show Your Caller ID

Sometimes you do not want the person you are calling to know your iPhone phone number. You can easily hide your number so it does not display on their screen.

1 Go to **Settings > Phone > Show My Caller ID**

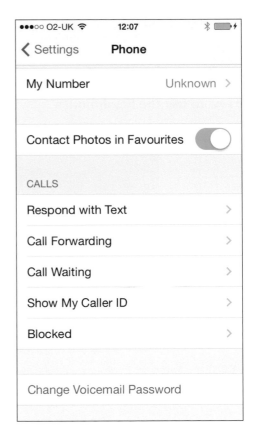

2 Tap Show My Caller ID **On** or **Off** depending on whether or not you want it to show

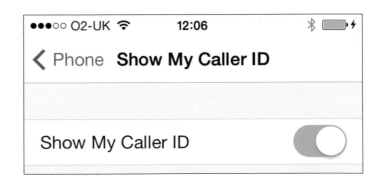

Call Forwarding

Sometimes you need to forward calls from your iPhone to another phone, for example, if you are somewhere with no cell phone coverage. This is pretty straightforward.

Setting up call forwarding

1 Go to **Settings > Phone > Call Forwarding**

2 Slide the **Call Forwarding** slider to the right (**On**)

3 You will be asked for the number you wish to use

4 When you no longer need to have your calls forwarded, go back and switch it off

Activate call forwarding if you cannot access the iPhone. You could forward to a landline or your PA.

Conference Calls

This allows you to talk to more than one person at a time and is much like making conference calls using a landline.

Make a conference call

1 Make a call

2 Tap the **Add Call** icon on the screen

3 The first call is put on hold

4 Tap **Merge Calls**

5 Now everyone can hear each other

6 Repeat until up to five people are on the same call

Visual Voicemail

This is a fantastic way to retrieve voicemail. No longer do you have to listen to irrelevant messages in order to hear the one you want. With Visual Voicemail you can tap the message you want to hear, and you can listen to that message and that message only.

To retrieve Visual Voicemail

1 Tap the **phone** icon at the bottom of the screen

2 Tap the **Voicemail** icon at the far right

3 View the voicemail messages

4 **Tap** the one you want to hear

5 To listen again, tap the **Play** icon

6 If you want to listen to an earlier part of the message, **drag the progress slider to the left**

7 You can call the caller back by tapping **Call Back**

8 You can tap the arrow to the right of the message and add the caller to your Contacts list, or add them to the favorites list

What happens if Visual Voicemail is not available?
This sometimes happens but it's easy to get your voicemail:

1 Tap **Phone > Keyboard**

2 Press and hold the **1** key

3 Retrieve your messages

Hot tip

Visual Voicemail makes it very easy to listen to specific voicemail messages.

Beware

Sometimes you cannot access Visual Voicemail (poor network signal). To retrieve your voicemails tap and hold "1" on the keypad.

Call Waiting

What is the value of call waiting? If call waiting is switched off, and someone phones you while you are on a call, they will be put straight through to voicemail. However, if call waiting is activated, they will know your line is busy and can wait until you are off the call. Or you can answer their call and put the first caller on hold.

1 Go to **Settings > Phone**

2 Tap **Call Waiting >**

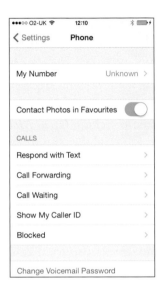

3 Slide the **Off** button to the **On** position

iPhone Usage Data

How many SMS messages do you have left this month? Or talk minutes? There are times when you need to monitor your usage, since exceeding your limits on your contracted allowance will cost you extra.

How can you check how much you have used?
The iPhone has Usage data under **Settings > General > Usage**. The information here is very limited and it does not tell you what you have used, or have left, in this month's cycle.

Third party applications
There are a number of apps that can track your monthly usage. These include *Optus Mobile Usage* for the US and *Allowance* for the UK. Other countries will have their own specific apps.

If you exceed your monthly allowance on the iPhone you will be charged extra.

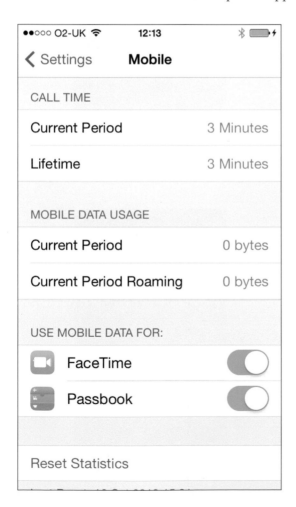

Third Party Apps for Usage

There are many apps for monitoring cellular and Wi-Fi data usage. One of these is Data Usage Monitor. Once you tell the app the billing data, it works out your usage for the month which will prevent you exceeding your data allowance. (If you are on unlimited data there's no need to worry!)

Hot tip

There are some great third party apps that help you monitor your monthly phone, text and data usage.

The app also comes with a useful built-in speed tester.

3 Messaging

Sending text and multimedia messages is no longer a chore. The iPhone carries out these functions effortlessly and this chapter shows how to use the Messages app for all of your messaging needs.

Text Messaging

Sending text messages on the iPhone 5s and 5c is a fast and efficient way to communicate using your iPhone. You can send messages as SMS (simple message system), MMS (multimedia message system – basically text with pictures), and iMessage.

SMS

Hot tip

You can send SMS, MMS and iMessages to multiple recipients.

Don't forget

SMS and MMS messages are sent over your mobile carrier's network. iMessages are sent to other Apple users with an Apple ID, using Wi-Fi.

1 Tap the **Messages** app on the Home screen

2 Tap the **New message** icon at the top right of the screen

3 Enter a **recipient name** or a phone number at the top

4 Add any other names if you wish to send to more than one person

5 Go to the **text box** at the bottom and enter your message

6 Hit **Send**

7   The progress bar will show you the status of the message

8   Once sent, your message will appear in a green speech bubble (blue if iMessage)

9   Once the recipient replies, you will see their message below yours in a white speech bubble

iMessage

You can send iMessages using cellular or Wi-Fi to other people with iOS devices (or Macs). Simply send your text in the usual way. You will know it's an iMessage rather than SMS because your message will be in a blue speech bubble. You can also check the status of your text message (delivered or read) by checking below your message.

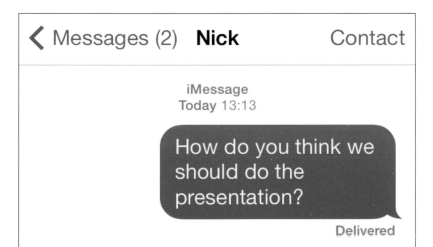

To see how many characters you have used go to **Settings > Messages > Character Count > On**. 160 characters is the limit for one SMS.

You can tell this message is an iMessage – you see iMessage at the top, plus my text is in a blue speech bubble. You can also see that my message was successfully delivered. If you see the **...** ellipsis in the speech bubble on the left, the person you texted is writing a reply.

If SMS Message Fails

Sometimes things go wrong, maybe you entered a wrong digit, and the message does not get sent. You have the option of retrying. You can also check the contact details and amend the number there.

1 Tap on the red exclamation mark

2 Tap on **Try Again**

Sending to Multiple Recipients

The Messages app allows you to send texts to more than one person. You can also send texts to groups of individuals.

Send SMS to multiple recipients

1 Type the **name** of the first recipient

2 A shaded block surrounds their name

3 Tap the **To:** field again and add a second name

4 Repeat this until all recipients are added

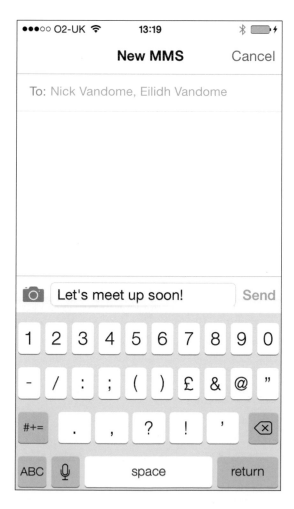

Text Message Sounds

Some people like silent texts, others prefer to feel a vibration, but most people like to hear their text messages arrive on the iPhone.

This is easy to set up

1 Tap **Settings**

2 Go to **Settings > Sounds**

3 Tap **Text Tone**

4 Select the **Text Tone** you want from the list

5 Or you can check **None**

Assign SMS messages a specific sound so you know you have received an SMS.

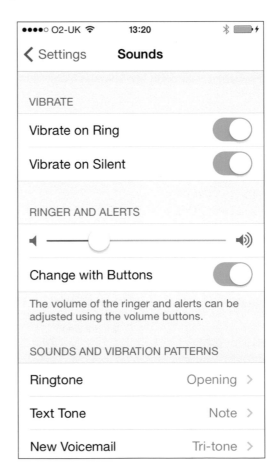

Message Settings

You can use the Message Settings to customize your text messaging exactly the way you want. To do this:

1 Open **Settings > Messages**

2 Drag the **iMessage** button to **On** to enable you to send iMessages to other Apple users on iPhones, iPad, iPod Touch and Mac computers

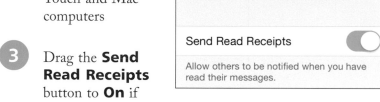

3 Drag the **Send Read Receipts** button to **On** if you want other people to be notified when you read their messages

4 Drag the **Send as SMS** button to **On** to enable you to send a SMS message if iMessage is unavailable. This will be done over your cellular network rather than with Wi-Fi, which is used for iMessages

5 Select the other settings as required, such as showing a **Subject Field** in a message

Sending MMS Messages

The iPhone can send more than just plain boring text messages. MMS means Multimedia Message Service, which is basically a means of sending images, including video, to a recipient, rather than a simple SMS message. Each MMS counts as two SMS messages, so be careful how many you send.

To send an MMS

1 Tap **Messages** and tap **New**

2 Enter the **name** of the recipient

3 Tap the **camera** icon (to the left of the text box)

4 Tap on the **Take Photo or Video** button to capture a new image, or tap on the **Choose Existing** button to select an image from your photos or videos

5 Browse to the picture or video you want to send, from within the **Photos** app, and tap on the **Choose** button to select it

6 The picture will appear in the message box

7 Type your text message to accompany the picture or video

8 Hit **Send**

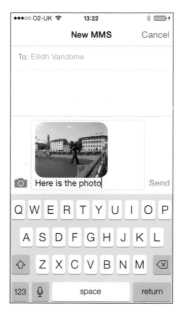

Managing Text Messages

Forwarding a text message
You can easily forward a text message to another person.

1 Open the message and press and hold on the message

2 Tap on the **More** button

3 Tap on the **Forward** button and enter a recipient name

Deleting a text message

1 Open Messages to show your list of text messages

2 Swipe the text message left to right then tap **Delete**

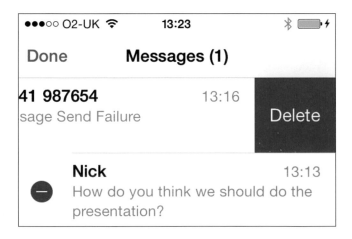

Editing text messages

You can selectively delete parts of a text message thread:

1 Open the message and press and hold on the message

2 Tap on the **More** button

3 Tap next to a message to select it

4 Tap on **Delete All** to delete the selected messages, or tap on the **Trash** icon

Tap on the **Delete All** button to delete all of the message in a conversation.

Other Messaging Clients

On the iPhone there are several apps that let you message friends and colleagues. Examples include Skype, WhatsApp, Viber, and others.

Skype

Viber

Using Skype

1 Get yourself a **Skype account** using your computer (**www.skype.com**)

2 Download the free **iPhone Skype app** from the App Store

3 Open the app and log in using your registered **Username** and **Password**

4 Your **Contacts List** will be displayed. You can choose to see only those online (makes the list shorter). Tap on the People button to view your contacts at any time

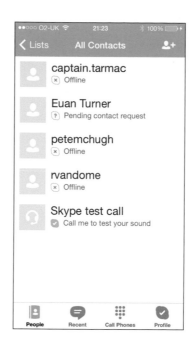

Tap on the **Call Phones** button on the bottom toolbar to access the keypad for typing a number, rather than selecting a contact that already has a number assigned to them.

5 Tap on a contact to make a voice, video or text call

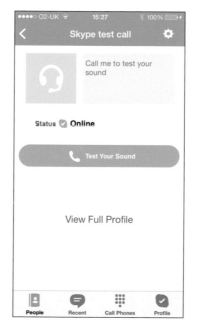

6 Tap on this button to add more contacts, either by adding them from your iPhone Contacts, or by searching on Skype

Live Links

When you send a text message, an email, or use a social networking app where text is inserted, you can add phone numbers, web URLs and email addresses. The recipient can then click on these to return the call, visit a website, or send an email.

SMS with telephone number

URLs, email addresses and phone numbers in messages, web pages and emails are live and can be tapped to call the number, view other web pages or send emails.

Tap on a phone number in a message to call it

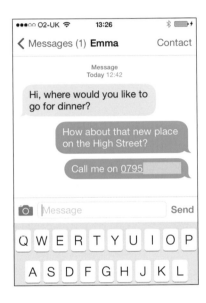

SMS with email address

Tap on an email address in a message to create an email to that person

Live links in emails

If you send an email to someone and include a website, email address or URL these are also clickable.

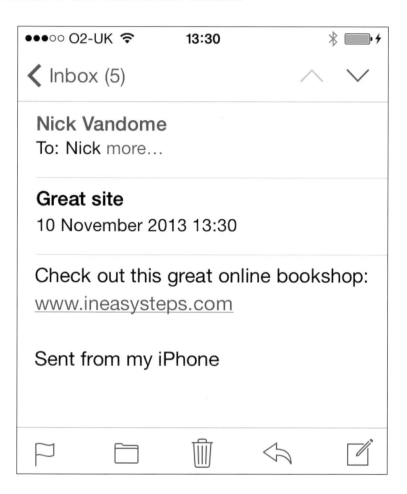

Click on the link to go to that site in a web browser.

Live Links in Safari

Live links to phone numbers and email addresses don't end with Mail. You can use phone numbers in Safari. If you see a number you want to dial on a web page, put your finger on the number and keep your finger there until a box pops up showing you the various options.

You can

- Call the number

- Send a text message

- Create a new contact

- Add to an existing contact

1 Put your finger on the number and keep it there

> **CUSTOMER SERVICES CONTACT**
>
> Opening Hours: Mon, Tues, Thurs, Fri
> 16.00 Wed: 10.00-16.00.
> Edinburgh Tel:
> ›› **0845 607 0161**
> Edinburgh Fax:
> ›› **0131 200 3932**
> Glasgow Tel:
> ›› **0845 607 0164**

2 You will see the various options

4 Audio & Video

The iPhone is a workhorse but is also a fun device, able to play audio and video just like an iPod. This chapter shows how to obtain, play and manage music on your iPhone and also work with video content.

The Music App

The music app can be used to turn your iPhone into your own personal jukebox. To use it:

1 Tap on the **Music** app on the Dock

2 Browse for music using the bottom toolbar in the Music app

Don't forget

If you don't like the way the various functions are shown on the Music app you can change these. Go to **Settings > Music**.

3 Tap on the **More** button to view more options, such as Composers

Playlist view

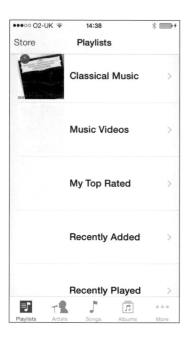

Songs view

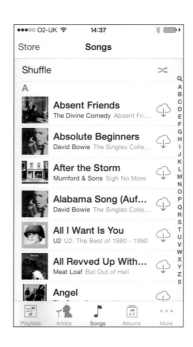

Artists view

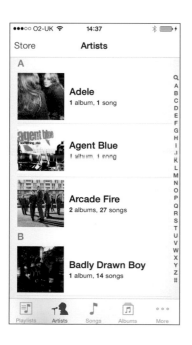

Genius view

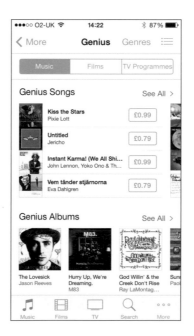

Don't forget

The Music app suggests songs and albums that it thinks go well together! They appear in Genius View.

Play Audio on the Music App

The Music app is very versatile for playing your favorite albums and tracks. To use it:

1 Tap on the **Music** app on the Dock

2 Tap **Artists** if you want to search this way, or choose **Playlists** or **Songs**

3 Tap the name of the artist

4 Choose the album you want to hear

5 Tap on the track that you want to play. If you select the first track of an album then the other tracks will play in sequence after it

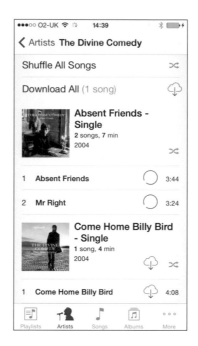

6 The selected track starts playing in the Music app interface

Music App Controls

Once a track is playing in the Music app there are a number of controls that can be used.

1 Tap once on the middle button to pause/play the currently-playing track. Use the buttons on either side to move to the beginning or end of a track

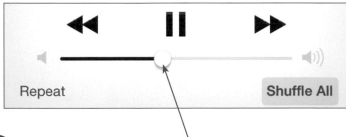

Repeat   Shuffle All

2 Drag this button to increase or decrease the volume

3 Tap once on this button to repeat a song or album after it has played

Repeat

4 Tap once on this button to shuffle the order of songs on your iPhone

Shuffle All

Cover View
In any view in the Music app, rotate your iPhone to landscape to view thumbnails of the albums on your phone.

Hot tip

Music controls, including Play, Fast Forward, Rewind and Volume can also be applied in the **Control Center**, which can be accessed by swiping up from the bottom of the screen.

View the Audio Tracks

Sometimes you want to see what tracks are available while you are listening to audio.

While viewing the album artwork screen

1 Tap the small **bullet list** icon at the top right of the screen

2 The album cover flips to show audio tracks available

3 To get back to the main screen again, tap on the **Done** button at the top right

Adjusting the Volume

There are several ways of increasing or decreasing the audio volume.

Headphones

Use the **+** and **−** on the headset.

Volume control switch on iPhone

Use the physical volume control on the iPhone.

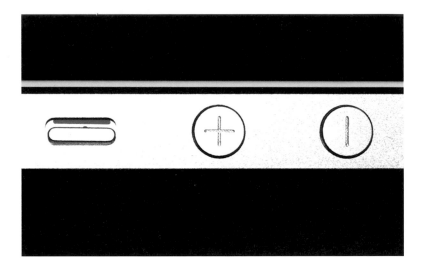

Hot tip

Even when you are using another app, you can still access your Music app controls by clicking the Home Button twice.

From the Music app screen

Move the circle right (increase volume) or left (to decrease).

Search for Audio

Sometimes you can't see the music or artist you are looking for. Hit the search tool at the top right of the Music app screen and type the name of the artist, album, song, podcast, or whatever you are looking for.

1 Tap on this bar to search for items in alphabetical order

You can search for audio or video in your Music app within the Music app itself, or you can use Spotlight.

2 Tap in the **Search** box and enter a song or artist. Tap on one of the results

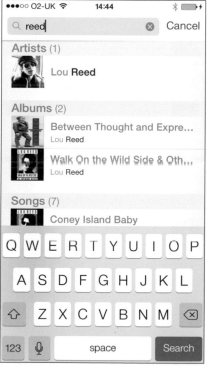

Creating Your Own Playlists

Using the Music app you can create your own playlists.

To set up your own playlist

1 Go to **Music > Playlists**

2 Tap **New Playlist...**

3 Name it and tap on the **Save** button

4 Tap the **+** icon to add songs

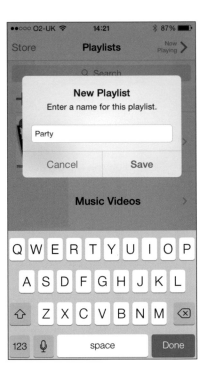

5 If you want to remove or edit the playlist, open the playlist and tap **Edit**

Buying Music

Music on the iPhone can be downloaded and played using the iTunes and the Music apps respectively. iTunes links to the iTunes Store, from where music, and other content, can be bought and downloaded to your iPhone. To do this:

1 Tap once on **iTunes Store** app

2 Tap once on the **Music** button on the iTunes toolbar at the bottom of the window

3 Use these buttons at the top of the window to view the music content, or swipe up and down, and left and right in the main window

4 Tap once on an item to view it. Tap once here to buy an album or tap on the button next to a song to buy that individual item

5 Purchased items are included in the Music app's Library

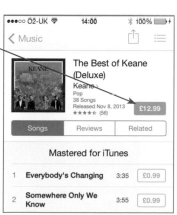

You need to have an Apple ID with credit or debit card details added to be able to buy music from the iTunes Store.

Watching Video

The iPhone is a great video player. Video now has its own app (it used to be within the Music app).

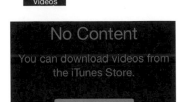

1 Tap on the **Videos** app

2 To find content, tap on the **Store** button

No Content
You can download videos from the iTunes Store.

Store

3 Browse the video store to select a title and download it

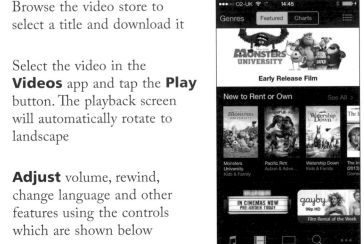

4 Select the video in the **Videos** app and tap the **Play** button. The playback screen will automatically rotate to landscape

5 **Adjust** volume, rewind, change language and other features using the controls which are shown below

6 If you want to stop, simply press the **Play/Pause** button and it will save your place

Hot tip

You can also watch YouTube videos on your iPhone, by either going to the YouTube website in Safari, or by downloading the YouTube app from the App Store.

Where to Obtain Videos

You have a few ways of getting videos on your iPhone:

- Home movies, either using a camcorder or the iPhone itself

- Convert your purchased DVDs to iPhone format

- Buy or rent movies from the iTunes store

iTunes Store

Select the video you wish to purchase or rent. Once downloaded, it will be added to the Movies window in iTunes. When you sync your iPhone, choose the movies you wish to sync.

Convert Your DVDs

There are several programs available for Mac and PC that will convert purchased DVDs into an iPhone-friendly format.

Handbrake

This is an open source application for Mac. Simply put your commercial DVD in the Mac optical disk drive, open Handbrake and choose the format for the Save. There is an iPhone-specific video format available.

Once converted, the video should be dropped onto the Movies tab of iTunes. In the iPhone Video tab make sure this video is checked so that the next time you sync the iPhone the video will be copied to the iPhone.

Handbrake for the Mac is a free DVD converter which has several save options, including iPhone.

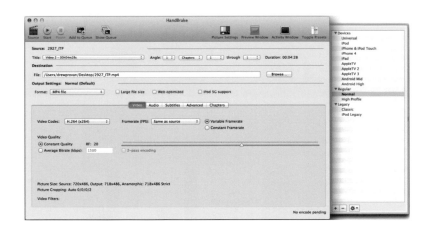

PC software for converting DVDs

There are many different programs for the PC, including Roxio Crunch.

Is it legal?

For a variety of reasons some DVDs may not convert properly, possibly through copy protection. In general, the copying of commercial DVDs, even for your own iPhone use, is not necessarily legal.

Podcasts

The iPhone is also great for listening to audiobooks and podcasts. This can be done with the Podcasts app that can be downloaded from the App Store.

1 Locate the Podcasts app in the App Store and download it (it is free)

2 Tap on the Podcasts app to open it and view the available podcasts (which can be audio and video)

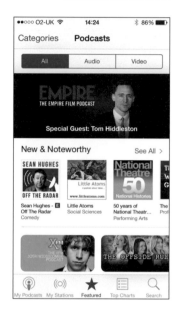

3 Tap on a podcast to download it to your iPhone

4 Tap on a podcast to listen to it. If a podcast has a red circle on it with a number, this means that there are updates available for it

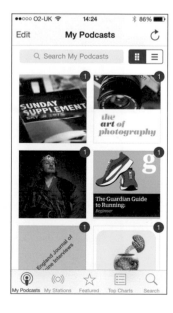

Play Music Using Siri

Siri voice recognition can find your music and play it.

1 **Press and hold the Home Button** until Siri opens

2 Say **Play ...** (*whatever song you want to play*)

3 Siri will find the song and start playing it

5 Photos & Video

The iPhone has a built-in camera, and is able to shoot movies as well as still images. In addition, you can even edit your photos and movies directly on the iPhone itself.

Sharing Content

Since the iPhone can store and create such a great range of content, it seems a shame to keep it all to yourself and there are options for sharing all kinds of content. The example here is for one of the most popular, sharing photos, but the process also applies to other content such as web pages, notes and contacts.

1 Open a photo at full size and tap on the **Share** button

2 Tap on one of the options for sharing the photo. These include messaging, emailing, sending to iCloud, adding to a contact in your Contacts app, using as your iPhone wallpaper, tweeting, sending to Facebook or Flickr, printing and copying the photo

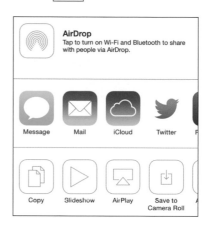

3 The photo is added to the item selected in Step 2, in this case an email

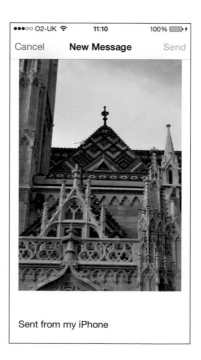

Sharing with AirDrop

AirDrop is a feature for sharing files wirelessly over short distances. It has been available on Mac computers for a number of years and it now comes to the iPhone 5s and 5c. To use it:

1 Swipe up from the bottom of the screen to open the Control Center, to activate AirDrop

2 Tap on the **AirDrop** link

3 Select how you want to share your files with other AirDrop user. This can be with your contacts in the Contacts app, or Everyone

4 Select an item you want to share, such as a photo in the Photos app, and tap on the **Share** button

5 If there are people nearby with AirDrop activated, the AirDrop button will be blue on your iPhone

6 Tap on an available icon to share your content with this person (they will have to accept it via AirDrop once it has been sent)

There have been some issues with AirDrop working properly on iOS devices. Make sure you are as close as possible to the other user and that they have AirDrop turned on in the Control Center. If it is a contact, make sure that you have their iCloud email in your Contacts app.

111

iPhone Camera

The camera in the iPhone can be used for taking still photographs and video.

Tap to Focus
The iPhone camera can adjust the focus and the exposure — by tapping the screen when taking a picture or shooting video.

Geotagging
The iPhone camera will provide geotagging data, including your geographical coordinates, provided you have switched Location Services on (**Settings > Privacy > Location Services**).

The camera has a resolution of 8 megapixels which is more than enough to take good pictures and video. The poorest results are seen when the lighting is low. Night shots are particularly bad. For best shots make sure there is lots of light around. The iPhone 5s and 5c also have a camera flash for the main camera. The main camera is the one on the back of the iPhone and is known as an iSight camera.

Location of camera lens
You will find this on the back of the iPhone at the top left corner. Take care not to scratch the lens, and clean the lens with a lint-free cloth, such as used for cleaning glasses.

Night shots, or scenes with reduced light, often produce poor quality images on the iPhone.

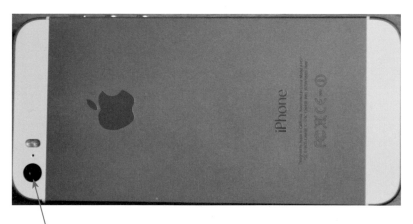

iSight camera lens

Still Images Using Main Camera

The iPhone camera can capture photos in various aspects
(Standard, Square and Panorama) and also capture video.

1 Tap the **Camera** icon to load the app

2 The shutter will open to show the image

3 Tap on the shutter button

4 The picture will be visible for a second or two before
being dropped into the folder called **Camera Roll**,
which you can find by launching the Photos app

5 Take care not to place your finger over the lens

Tap on the Filters button
before you take a photo
to use a selection of
filter effects that can be
applied to the photo.

Where Are My Pictures?

Once photos have been captured they can be viewed and organized in the Photos app. To do this:

1 Tap on the **Photos** app

2 At the top level, all photos are displayed according to the years in which they were taken

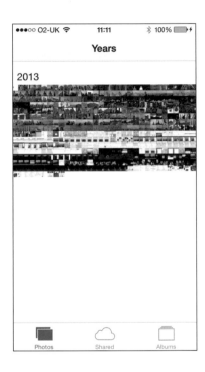

Hot tip

If you have iCloud set up, all of your photos will also be saved under the **My Photo Stream** button in the **Albums** section. This enables all of your photos to be made available on any other iCloud-enabled devices.

114

Don't forget

Tap once on the **Photos**, **Shared** and **Albums** buttons at the bottom of the **Years**, **Collections** or **Moments** windows, to view the photos in each of these sections.

3 Tap within the **Years** window to view photos according to specific, more defined, timescales. This is the **Collections** level. Tap on the **Years** button to move back up one level

4 Tap within the **Collections** window to drill down further into the photos, within the **Moments** window. Tap on the **Collections** button to go back up one level

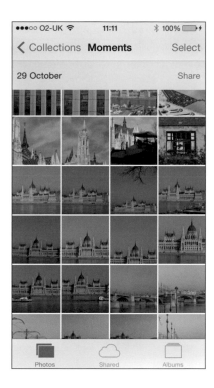

Moments are created according to the time at which the photos were added or taken: photos added at the same time will be displayed within the same Moment.

5 Tap on a photo within the **Moments** window to view it at full size. Tap on the **Moments** button to go back up one level

Double-tap with one finger on an individual photo to zoom in on it. Double-tap with one finger again to zoom back out. To zoom in to a greater degree, swipe outwards with thumb and forefinger.

Creating Albums

Within the Photos app it is possible to create different albums in which you can store photos. This can be a good way to organize them according to different categories and headings. To do this:

1 Tap on the **Albums** button

2 Tap on this button

3 Enter a name for the new album

4 Tap on the **Save** button

New Album
Enter a name for this album.

Budapest

Cancel   Save

Don't forget

When photos are placed into albums the originals remain in the main **Photos** section.

5 Tap on the photos you want to include in the album

6 Tap on the **Done** button

Done

●●●○○ O2-UK 🔶   11:33   ✳ 100% ▭ ✦

Add 96 photos to "Budapest".

❮ Collections **Moments**   Done

25 October   Select

26–27 October   Deselect

7 Tap on the **Albums** button to view the album

Budapest
96   ❯

Selecting Photos

It is easy to take hundreds, or thousands, of digital photos and most of the time you will only want to use a selection of them. Within the Photos app it is possible to select individual photos so that you can share them, delete them or add them to albums.

1 Access the Moments section and tap on **Select** button

Hot tip

Press and hold on a photo to access an option to copy it, rather than selecting it.

2 Tap on the photos you want to select, or tap on the **Select** button again to select all of the photos

Don't forget

To add items to an album, tap on this button in the **Moments** section.

Tap on photos to select them, then tap on the **Add To** button and select either an existing album or tap on the **New Album** link to create a new album with the selected photos added to it.

3 Tap on the **Deselect** button if you want to remove the selection

4 Use these buttons to, from left to right, share the selected photos, delete them or add them to an album

Editing Photos

The Photos app has options to perform some basic photo-editing operations. To use these:

1 Open a photo at full-screen size and tap once on the **Edit** button

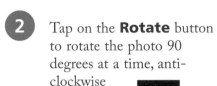

Use the Red-Eye editing option to remove red-eye for people by tapping on the affected red-eye area.

2 Tap on the **Rotate** button to rotate the photo 90 degrees at a time, anti-clockwise

118

Editing changes are made to the original photo once the changes have been saved. These will also apply to any albums into which the photo has been placed.

3 Tap on the **Enhance** button to have auto-coloring editing applied to the photo

4 Tap on the **Filters** button to select special effects to be applied to the photo

5 Tap on the **Crop** button and drag the resizing handles to select an area of the photo that you want to keep and discard the rest

Most photos benefit from some cropping, to enhance the main subject and give it greater prominence.

6 For each function, tap once on the **Save** button to save the photo with the selected changes

7 Tap on this button to **Cancel** the whole editing process

Taking Videos

To capture your own video footage:

1 Tap the **Camera** icon to load the app. The shutter will open to show the image

2 Drag just above the shutter button until **Video** is showing

3 Tap on the red **Record** button

Hot tip

Videos are located in the Camera Roll album.

4 The **Record** button turns into a red square during filming

5 When you have finished, tap the Record button again. Your video will be in the Camera Roll Album

Editing the Video

You can edit the video you have taken on a Mac, PC or directly on the iPhone itself.

1 Tap the **Photos** app

2 Tap **Camera Roll** and locate your video

3 **Tap the video** to open it – the image can be viewed in portrait or landscape, but landscape is easier for trimming

4 **Touch the screen** and the trimming timeline will be shown at the top of the screen

5 Decide what (if anything) you want to trim and drag the sliders on the left and right until you have marked the areas you wish to trim

Video editing is now non-destructive which means you can trim your video, but the original video clip is left intact.

6 Tap the blue **trim** icon at the top right of the screen and the unwanted video will be removed

Panoramic Photos

You can now take panoramic shots where you pan across a scene and the iPhone stitches the images together to give a very wide photo which would be impossible to take using the standard camera settings.

1 Open the **Camera** and select **Pano**

2 Once you tap the photo icon (bottom of screen) you need to **pan from left to right keeping the arrow on the center line** for best results

3 Once the arrow reaches the right side, the software will generate the panoramic image which will be saved to your Camera Roll

6 The Standard Apps

Each iPhone comes pre-installed with a

core set of applications, which make

the iPhone so versatile and useful.

In this section we explore the apps that

haven't been covered in other chapters and

show how to get the best use out of them.

Calendar

For people who want to get organized, people in business, education and many other sectors, the core applications are: Calendar, Mail, Contacts, Phone and Notes.

These apps integrate well with each other on the iPhone and also the PC and Mac.

Setting up Calendar

Before you start entering data into Calendar, there are one or two settings you should check:

1 Go to **Settings > Mail, Contacts, Calendars**

2 Tap **Mail, Contacts, Calendars** to open

3 Scroll down the page until you find **Calendars**

4 Switch **New Invitation Alerts** to **On**

Make sure your Time Zone is set correctly or all your appointments will be incorrect.

5 Choose what to **Sync** (Do you want all events or just those for the past two weeks, month, three months, or six months?)

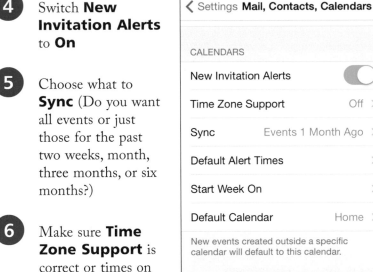

Turn Calendars **On** in iCloud (**Settings > iCloud**) to ensure your calendar events are saved to iCloud and so will be available on other iCloud-enabled devices.

6 Make sure **Time Zone Support** is correct or times on your calendar will be incorrect

7 Set your **Default calendar** – when you make new appointments using Calendar this is where the appointments will be added (You can add to another calendar quite easily, though.)

Calendar Views

To start using the Calendar:

1 Tap the **Calendar** icon to open the app

2 You will see the **Month View** – if it opens in **Day** or **List**, tap on the **Month** name at the top of the screen

3 This shows an overview of the month

4 A gray dot means you have an appointment on that day, but it does not tell you how long the appointment is or what it is. But tap on the dot and you will see what the day's appointments are

5 If you need a detailed view of your appointments, check out the **Day** view (see next page)

Back one year   Today

Dots represent appointments

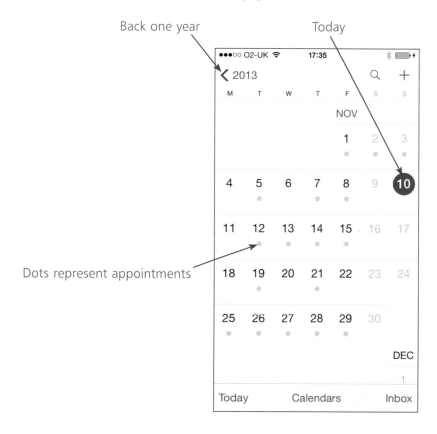

Hot tip

The Calendar uses continuous scrolling to move through Month view. This means you can view weeks across different months, rather than just viewing each month in its entirety, i.e. you can view the second half of one month and the first half of the next one in the same calendar window.

Day View

This provides a more detailed view of your day, showing the times on the left margin, and all your appointments are shown in the colors chosen by you.

Tap on a day to view its details in the panel below

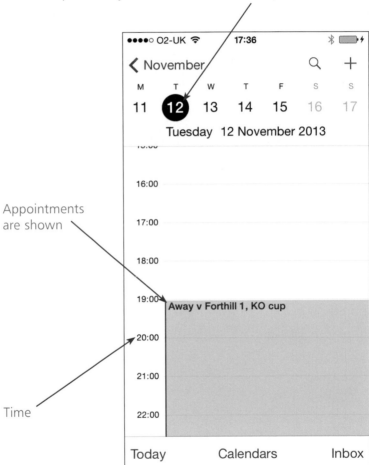

Swipe up and down on a day to view the different time slots.

Appointments are shown

Time

Tap on the **Today** button to go to the current day

Swipe left and right to view different days

List View

Sometimes you want to see all your appointments as a list, rather than browsing through several months' worth of appointments using the other views.

Simply tap on the **Search** icon at the top of the page and you will see every appointment, with the earliest at the top and the latest at the bottom.

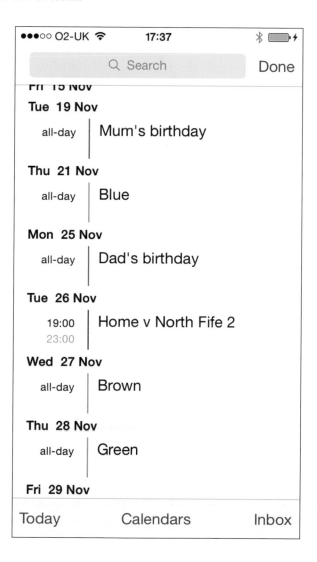

Flick up and down until you find what you want

Searching Calendar

It's very easy to find appointments using the Search function within Calendar. You can also use Spotlight Search to find appointments.

1 Tap **Calendar** to open

2 Tap **List view**

3 Tap the **Search box** for an item, e.g. Blue. After you enter a few letters the appointments containing those letters will appear below

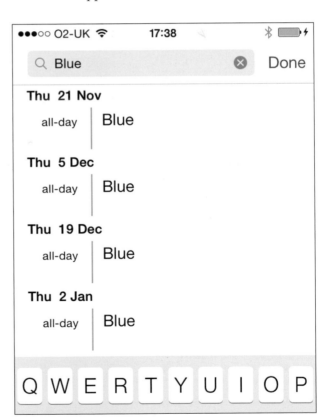

Don't forget

You can search your calendar using the inbuilt search tool or use Spotlight.

4 Tap a found appointment to see its details

Spotlight Search

You can also search for appointments using the iPhone Spotlight Search. To do this:

1 Swipe downwards anywhere on the Home screen to access the Spotlight Search

2 Enter a search word or phrase. This will search over all of the content on your iPhone, including within Calendars

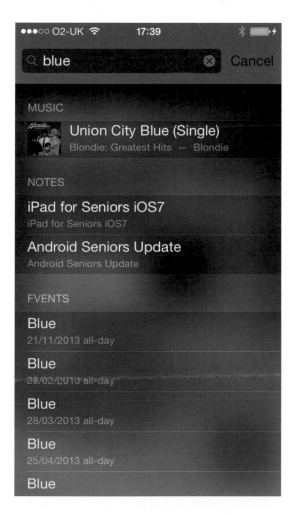

3 Tap on one of the entries under the **Events** heading in the search results

Adding Appointments

Set up new appointment

To create a new appointment, or event, in the Calendar app:

1 Tap once on this button to create a new event or press and hold on a time slot

2 Enter a Title and a Location for the event

3 Drag the **All-day** button to Off to set a timescale for the event

4 Tap on the **Starts** button and drag on the barrels to set the time at which the appointment will start

5 Do the same for the **Ends** time for the appointment

6 Tap on the **Alert** button and select a time at which you want an alert about the appointment

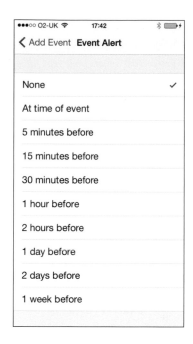

7 Tap on the **Calendar** button and select a calendar on which you would like the appointment to be included

8 Tap on the **Repeat** button and select a time for when you want the appointment or event to be repeated. This is a good option for items such as birthdays

Set up your repeat items, such as birthdays and anniversaries.

Notes App

All good smartphones have some kind of note-taking software and the iPhone is no exception. The Notes application can be found on the Home page, but you can move it to wherever you want it. The notes you make can be synced with your desktop computer and we will look at this later.

To make a note

1 Tap the **Notes** icon to open the application

2 All of your notes will be displayed. Tap on one to access it and edit it

3 Tap the **New** button to make a new note

●●●○○ O2-UK 🛜	17:46	❋ 🔋✦
‹ Folders		New
Book order		17:46 ›
iPhone 5 iOS 7		17:45 ›
Checklist for books		17:45 ›
Mac Computing Ma...		Yesterday ›
Elements 12		Tuesday ›
OS X Mavericks		24/10/2013 ›
Windows 8.1		21/10/2013 ›
Elements 12		17/10/2013 ›

4 Enter content for the note. The first line will become the note's title

5 Tap **Done** when you are finished

6 Tap on the **Notes** button to go back to list view of all of your notes

7 Use the buttons on the bottom toolbar to, from left to right, share a note, delete it or create another new note

Maps App

Maps is a great application – it can help you find where you are now, where you want to go, help you plan the route, tell you which direction you are facing and where all the traffic is.

Hot tip

Satellite view can also be used for the Flyover feature, if this is available for the selected area.

Hot tip

To see which way you are facing, tap the search icon (bottom left) until it shows a blue beam.

Don't forget

Maps will only work with its full functionality if Location Services is switched On.

Open maps, you are here

Tap the blue circle to view details

Press and hold to drop a pin

Satellite view

Satellite 3D view

Finding a route

Tap the Directions button and enter your start and end points.

Maps will calculate a route. It will also tell you how long it will take by car, public transport and by foot.

1 By default, your current direction is used for the **Start** field. If you want to change this, tap and enter a new location or address

2 Enter a destination (**End**) location or address

3 Tap on the **Route** button on the keyboard (or at the top of the Directions window)

4 The route is shown on the map

5 Tap on the **Start** button to get directions

6 The route is shown on the map with directions for each section. As you follow the directions they will change for the next step of the journey

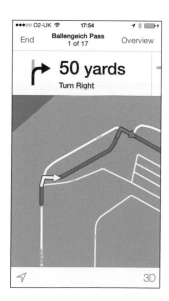

The Google Maps app is a good alternative that can be downloaded to your iPhone 5. It includes voice-guided, turn-by-turn navigation, live traffic conditions and information on public transport. Google claims to constantly keep the "map of the world" updated!

Weather App

This app tells you what the weather forecast is for the next six days. You can program the app to show the weather in multiple places. You can also choose between Centigrade or Fahrenheit.

Tap on this button to select different locations

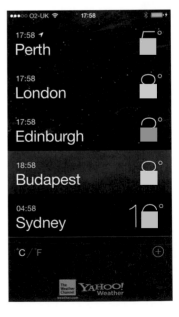

Stocks & Passbook

The Stocks app makes it easy to see how your stocks and shares are doing, both numerically and graphically.

What's happening on the stock market. (You can add your own stocks to see how they are performing each day.)

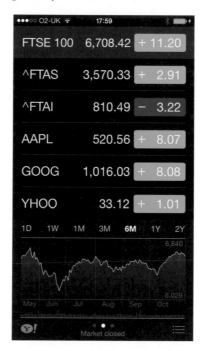

Passbook stores your boarding passes and other coupons. You need to purchase additional software using the App Store to make Passbook fully functional.

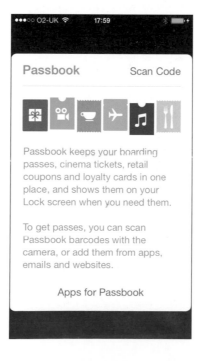

iBooks

This is a "standard" app but won't be on your iPhone by default. You need to go and grab a copy from the app store (free). You will need to have an iTunes account, even to download free books.

Download the iBooks app and tap on it to view your library.

Newsstand is very similar to iBooks, but can be used to download and read magazines and newspapers instead of books.

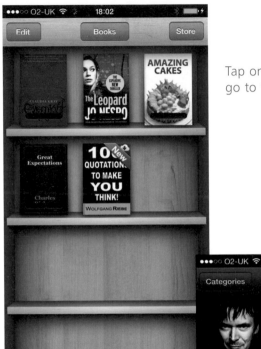

Tap on the **Store** button to go to the iBooks Store.

View, preview and download new books to read on your iPhone. These will be placed in the iBooks Library (above).

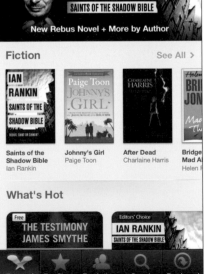

Game Center

For all gaming fans, this app can be used to download and play games from the App Store and also play against other people in multi-player games and compare your scores and achievements with other players.

1 Tap on the Game Center app to view your own gaming details. You have to log in with your Apple ID to use Game Center and all of its features

2 Use the bottom toolbar to access games and also add friends so that you can compete against them and compare scores

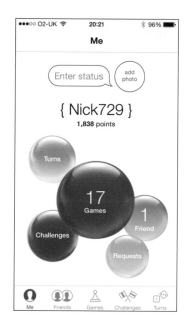

3 Tap on the **Games** button to view the games that you have within Game Center and also download more from the App Store

Calculator

As expected, this is a fully-functioning calculator. You can view a standard calculator if you view in portrait mode. However, if you rotate the screen to landscape, the calculator changes to a scientific calculator.

Rotate through 90° to see the scientific calculator:

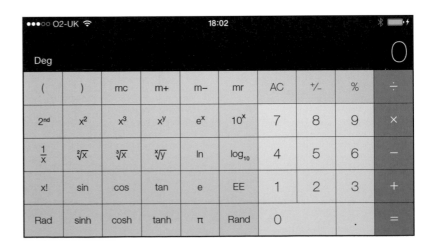

Clock

This app functions as a clock, alarm, stop watch and timer. You can see what time it is in any city in the world by adding these to your clock screen.

World clocks

Add more clocks

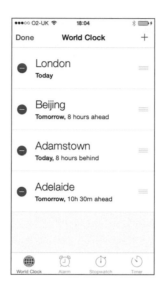

Alarm

Timer

Stopwatch

Compass

The compass needs to be calibrated before you use it – tilt the iPhone to do this. The red needle points to north and you can find your current location by allowing the compass to use your location when you start using it.

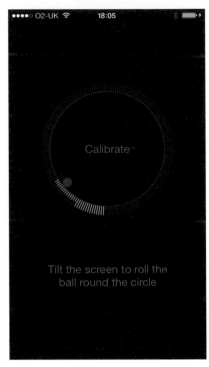

iTunes Store App

This is the iPhone version of the iTunes store on the Mac or PC. You can buy audio and video content for your iPhone.

Music

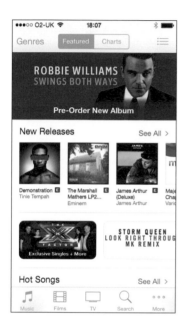

Movies

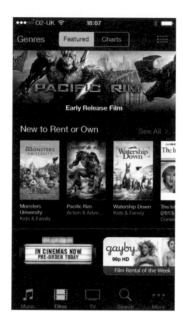

Don't forget

You must have an Apple ID to access the iTunes Store and register credit or debit card details in order to buy content from the store.

TV Shows

Audiobooks

Reminders

iOS 7 includes Reminders, a simple to-do list app that be used to save details about important events, meetings or simply items of shopping to buy. Reminders can be stored in the iCloud.

Using Reminders

1 Tap **Reminders** to open the app

2 Tap the **+** button to add a new Reminder (or just tap on a line)

3 The keyboard will appear. Type the name of your reminder

4 Tap the **i** button if you want to add more details

Location-based Reminders

You can ask Reminders to alert you when you are leaving or arriving at a location. For example, you might want to pick up your dry cleaning when you are near that location. By entering the zip code, Reminders will know where you are and if you are near the dry cleaners it will remind you to pick up your dry cleaning.

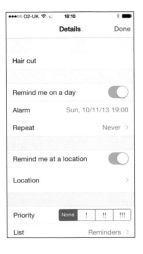

Siri

Siri is the voice recognition assistant that can make appointments, find items on your iPhone, open apps, get directions to locations, open Passbook, post to Facebook, send tweets and more.

To use Siri

1 Hold the **Home button** down until Siri appears

2 Speak your instructions clearly, e.g. *Call John, directions to nearest garage, what is the weather like tomorrow, open Safari*

3 Siri will show you what it thinks you said, and will carry out the operation. Tap on one of the results to view it

Notification Center

Although the Notification Center feature is not an app in its own right, it can be used to display information from a variety of apps. These appear as a list for all of the items you want to be reminded about or be made aware of. Notifications are set up within the Settings app. To do this:

1 Tap on the **Settings** app

2 Tap on the **Notification Center** tab

3 Drag the **Notifications View** and **Today View** buttons to **On** under the **Access on Lock Screen** heading. This will enable these items to be viewed even when the iPhone is locked

4 Drag the buttons to **On** for the items you want in the **Today View** of the Notification Center

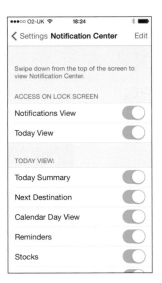

5 Tap on the items under the **Include** section to add items to appear in the Notification Center, under the **All** heading

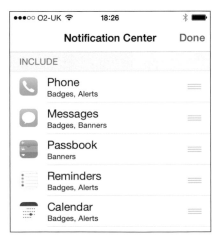

Once the Notification Center settings have been selected, it can be used to keep up-to-date with all of your important appointments and reminders. It can also be used to display the weather for your current location. To view the Notification Center from any screen:

1 Drag down from the top of any screen to view the Notification Center. Tap on the **Today** button to view the Weather summary, Calendar, items, Reminder items, and a summary of items for the next day

2 Swipe up the page to view all of the items. Tap on one to open it in its own default app

Swipe up on this button to close the Notification Center.

3 Tap on the **All** button to view notifications from all of the selected apps in Step 4 on the previous page

4 Tap on the **Missed** button to view notifications that have not been actioned in any way

Voice Memos

The iPhone is a great voice recorder. You can make voice notes for yourself then email them to colleagues or yourself to listen to later.

1 Tap **Voice Memos** to open

2 Tap the red **Record** button (it changes to a Pause icon). You will see the time elapsed

3 Pause recording by hitting the **Pause** button

4 When finished, tap the **Done** button

5 Give your voice memo a name and tap on the **OK** button

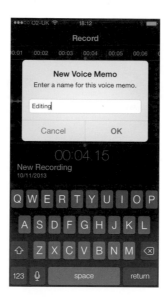

6 You can send a memo to someone, using the **Share** button. Tap on it to share the selected memo

7 Select the method for sharing the memo

Photos

This was covered, in part, in Chapter 5 and enables you to view your photos using the Years, Collections and Moments interface.

Use the **Share** button in the Photos app to share photos by Message, email, Twitter, Facebook and also send them to iCloud for storage, backup and sharing.

7 Web Browsing

Browsing the web on the iPhone is very easy using Apple's inbuilt browser, Safari. This chapter looks at how to use Safari, navigate around web pages, save and organize bookmarks and use live links within web pages.

Network Connections

Your iPhone can download data, such as emails and web pages, using a number of different types of connection. Some types of connection are faster than others. In general, Wi-Fi and Bluetooth should be kept off if you are not using them because they use a considerable amount of power.

GPRS
This is a slow network! But often better than nothing.

EDGE
This is a relatively slow connection but is fine for email.

3G and 4G
These are faster connections than EDGE. 4G is pretty close to Wi-Fi speed.

Wi-Fi connection
Joining a wireless connection will give you fairly fast download speeds. There are many free Wi-Fi hotspots. You can use home Wi-Fi once you enter the password.

Bluetooth
This is a short-range wireless connection, generally used for communication using a Bluetooth headset.

What do the various icons mean?
Look at the top of the iPhone and you will see various icons relating to cellular and other networks.

●●●●○	Signal strength
O2-UK	Network provider
📶	Wi-Fi On, with good signal strength
✳	Bluetooth On
✈	Airplane mode On
❋	iPhone is busy connecting, or getting mail, or some other task which has not completed

Beware

Wi-Fi and Bluetooth drain battery power. Switch off when not required.

Configuring Networks

Wi-Fi

1 Go to **Settings > Wi-Fi**

2 Tap **Wi-Fi**

3 Tap **On** if it is off

4 Choose a **network** from those listed and enter the password

5 Tap **Ask to Join Networks** if you want to be prompted each time a new network is found. It's generally easier to leave this **Off**

6 If you want to forget the network (e.g. maybe you have used one in a hotel), tap the name of the network you have joined, and tap **Forget this Network**

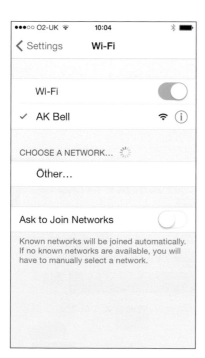

Browse with Safari

The Safari app is the default web browser on the iPhone. This can be used to view web pages, save favorites and read pages with the Reader function. To start using Safari:

1 Tap on the **Safari** app

2 Tap on the Address Bar at the top of the Safari window. Type a web page address

3 Tap on the **Go** button on the keyboard to open the web page

4 Also, suggested options appear as you type. Tap on one of these to go to that page

Don't forget

When a page opens in Safari a blue status bar underneath the page name indicates the progress of the loading page.

5 The selected web page opens in Safari

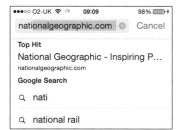

154

6 Swipe up and down and left and right to navigate around the page

Double-tap with one finger to zoom in on a page by a set amount. Double-tap with one finger to return to normal view. If the page has been zoomed by a greater amount by pinching, double-tap with two fingers to return to normal view.

7 Swipe outwards with thumb and forefinger to zoom in on a web page (pinch inwards to zoom back out)

Zooming & Scrolling

Because of the small screen, there is a limit to how much of the web page you can see.

Scroll
Place your finger on the screen and drag up or down, and left or right.

Zoom

1 Place your index and middle finger on the screen

2 Push them apart to zoom in

3 Pinch them together to zoom out

Don't forget

You can also zoom in by placing two fingers on the screen and pushing them apart (pull them closer to reduce the size).

Hot tip

Scroll up to the top of a page to activate the top address bar and the bottom toolbar when you tap on the page.

Add Web Clip to Home Screen

If you find a site that you want to revisit, but not add to bookmarks, you can add it to the Home screen:

1 Open the required web page

Add regularly-visited websites to your Home screen to save you having to look for the bookmark.

2 Tap on the **Share** button and tap on the **Add to Home Screen** button

3 Give the page a name and tap on the **Add** button

4 The web clip is added to the Home screen as an icon

Navigating Pages

When you are viewing pages within Safari there are a number of functions that can be used:

1 Tap on these buttons to move forward and back between web pages that have been visited

2 Tap here to view Bookmarked pages, Reading List pages and Shared Links

3 Tap here to add a bookmark, add to a reading list, add an icon to your iPhone Home screen, email a link to a page, tweet a page, send it to Facebook or print a page

4 Tap here to add a new tab

5 Tap on a link on a page to open it. Tap and hold to access additional options, to open in a new tab, add to a Reading List or copy the link

6 Tap and hold on an image and tap on **Save Image** or **Copy**

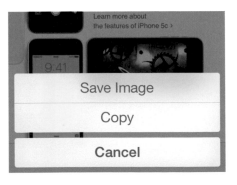

Tap and hold on the **Forward** and **Back** buttons to view lists of previously-visited pages in these directions.

If a web page has this button in the Address/Search box it means that the page can be viewed with the **Reader** function. This displays the page as text only, without any of the accompanying design to distract from the content. Tap on the button so that it turns black to activate the Reader.

Opening New Tabs

Safari supports tabbed browsing, which means that you can open separate pages within the same window and access them by tapping on each tab at the top of the page:

1 Tap here to open a new tab for another page

2 Open a new page by entering a web address into the Address Bar, or tap on one of the thumbnails in the **Favorites** window

3 Tap on the tab button in Step 1 to the view open tabs. Tap on one to go to that tab

4 Tap on this button to create a new tab (using the Favorites window in Step 2)

5 Tap on the cross on a tab to close it

The items that appear in the Favorites window can be determined within **Settings > Safari** and tapping once on the **Favorites** link.

Tap on the Private button in the tabs window to open an inPrivate browsing session, where no web details will be recorded.

Bookmarking Pages

Once you start using Safari you will soon build up a collection of favorite pages that you visit regularly. To access these quickly they can be bookmarked so that you can then go to them in one tap. To set up and use bookmarks:

1 Open a web page that you want to bookmark. Tap once here to access the sharing options

2 Tap on the **Bookmark** button

3 Tap on this link and select whether to include the bookmark on the Favorites Bar or in a Bookmarks folder

4 Tap on the **Save** button

5 Tap here to view all of the bookmarks. The Bookmarks folders are listed. Tap on the **Edit** button to delete or rename the folders

Reading List and Shared Links

The button in Step 5 on the previous page can be used to access your Reading List and Shared Links.

Reading List
This is a list of web pages that have been saved for reading at a later date. The great thing about this function is that the pages can be read even when you are offline and not connected to the Internet.

 1 Tap on this button to view your **Reading List**

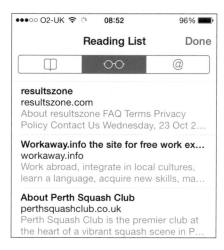

 Reading List items can be added from the Share button in Step 1 on the previous page.

Shared Links
If you have added a Twitter account on your iPhone you will be able to view your updates from the Shared Links button.

 1 Tap on this button to view your **Shared Links** updates

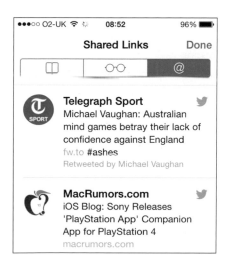

If you have accounts with Facebook or Twitter, you can link to these from the left-hand panel of the **Settings** app. Once you have done this you can share content to these sites from apps on your iPhone.

Safari Settings

Settings for Safari can be specified in the Settings app. To do this:

1 Tap on the **Settings** app

2 Tap on the **Safari** tab

3 Tap on the **Search Engine** link to select a default search engine to use

4 Tap on the default search engine you want to use with Safari

Beware

Don't use **Autofill** for names and passwords for any sites with sensitive information, such as banking sites, if other people have access to the iPhone.

5 Tap here for options for filling in online forms

Passwords & AutoFill   >

6 Tap on this button to access options for opening new links on a web site

Open Links   In New Page >

7 Tap on this button to access options for the Favorites window that appears when you open a new tab

Favorites   Favorites >

8 Drag the **Do Not Track** button to Off to disable this. If tracking is Off then no information will be recorded about visited websites

PRIVACY & SECURITY

Do Not Track

Block Cookies From third parties... >

9 Tap on the **Block Cookies** link to specify how Safari deals with cookies from websites

10 Tap on **Clear History** and **Clear Cookies and Data** to remove these items

Clear History

Clear Cookies and Data

11 Drag this button to **On** to enable alerts for when you have visited a fraudulent website

Fraudulent Website Warning

12 Drag this button to **On** to block pop-up messages

Block Pop-ups

Don't forget

Cookies are small items from websites that obtain details from your browser when you visit a site. The cookie remembers the details for the next time you visit the site.

Beware

If the **History** is cleared then there will be no record of any sites that have been visited.

Tricks

Fast Safari Scrolling

You can scroll up and down through web pages in Safari using your finger to flick up and down. But there is a very quick way of getting to the top of any web page.

Tap the time! (this works with text messages too).

Keyboard shortcuts when entering URLs

You don't need to type *.co.uk* or *.com*. On the Safari keyboard, press and hold the *.com* key. Alternatives will pop up (the *.kr* options are showing because the Korean keyboard is active).

Hot tip

You don't have to enter ".com" or ".co. uk" – simply hold down the ".com" key and alternatives will pop up.

8 Email

Most of us spend a great deal of time reading and composing emails. This chapter looks at how to set up email on your iPhone so that you can send and receive emails with your friends, family and colleagues.

Setting Up Email

The iPhone handles email well, and works with iCloud and Microsoft Exchange. It handles POP3, IMAP and can work with Yahoo! Mail, Google Mail and AOL.

Setting up an email account

You can link to a variety of email accounts and this example uses a Gmail account:

Don't forget

The iPhone can handle many types of email account. IMAP accounts are useful since you can see all your folders on the server, and can save email to specific folders easily.

1 Go to **Settings > Mail, Contacts, Calendars**

2 Tap on the **Add Account** button

3 Select the account you want to add (in this case Google)

Don't forget

If you set up an iCloud account you will automatically be given an iCloud email account.

4 Enter the account details and tap on the **Next** button

5 Select the items you want to include in the account and tap on the **Save** button

Deleting an account

To delete an emaill account from your iPhone:

1 Go to **Settings > Mail, Contacts, Calendars**

2 Tap on the account you want to delete

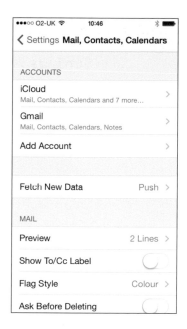

3 In the account window, swipe down to the bottom of the screen and tap on the **Delete Account** button

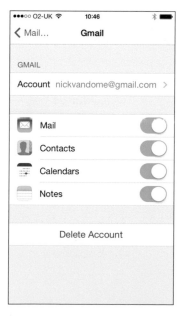

167

Using Exchange Server

Mail can collect email, and sync calendars and contacts using Microsoft Exchange Server, which is great news for businesses. To do this:

1 Go to **Settings > Mail, Contacts, Calendars**

2 Tap on the **Exchange** button

3 Enter the details of your Exchange account (you may need to get these from your IT Administrator) and tap on the **Next** button

Email Viewing Settings

As with other apps, there are a number of settings for email:

1 Go to **Settings > Mail, Contacts, Calendars**

2 Tap on one of the accounts to view its settings

3 Adjust settings for **Preview, Ask Before Deleting, Show To/Cc Label**, etc.

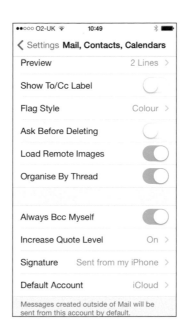

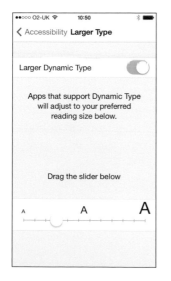

Hot tip

If you want to see more text on the screen set the font size to small.

4 Access **Settings > General > Accessibility > Larger Type** to change the text size

Composing Email

You can keep in touch with everyone, straight from the Mail app:

1 Tap the **Mail** icon to open the app

2 Tap an **email account** to open it

3 Tap the **New Email** icon (bottom right). A new email will open

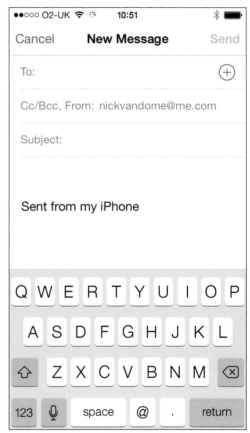

4 Tap the **To:** field and type the name of the recipient

5 Tap the **Subject:** and enter a subject for the email

6 Tap the **email body** area (below Subject:) and start typing your email

7 Insert a photo by selecting from **Photos** (touch and hold until you see **Copy** then touch and hold finger on email body until you see **Paste**). You can do the same with images in other apps, e.g., Safari

8 Once complete, hit **Send**

Reading Email

When you receive email you can view it in the Mail app:

1 Check the **Mail** icon for fresh mail – represented by a red circle. The number refers to the number of unread emails

2 Tap **Mail** to open

Hot tip

Flag important emails so you can find them again easily. Tap the Flag icon (bottom left of an open email message).

3 Tap the **Inbox** to open the email and if there is blue dot next to an email it means that it is unread

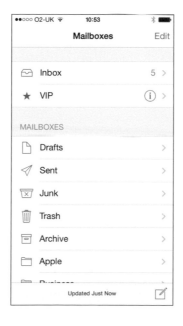

Don't forget

The paperclip icon shows you have received an attachment with an email.

...cont'd

Often, attachments do not download automatically. Tap the icon and you will see the attachment downloading. After downloading, tap to open.

To save a photo from an email, touch and hold the photo until you see Save Image. Tap this, and the photo will be added to the Camera Roll.

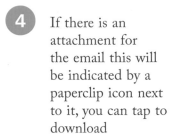

4 If there is an attachment for the email this will be indicated by a paperclip icon next to it, you can tap to download

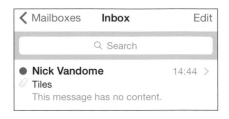

5 The attachment will appear in the body of the email. Tap on it to download it within the email

6 When the image attachment has finished downloading it will be visible in the body of the email

Forwarding Email

Once you have received an email you can reply to the sender, or forward it to someone else:

1 Open an email

2 Tap the **Reply/ Forward** icon at the bottom right of the screen

3 Select **Forward**

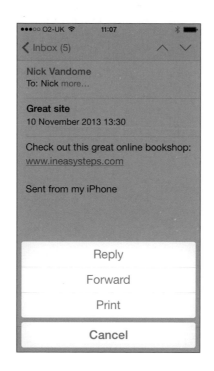

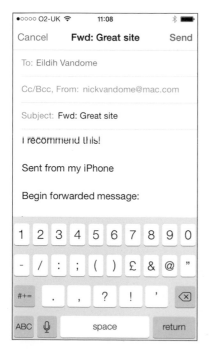

4 Enter the name of the recipient in the **To** box

5 In the body of the email, enter any message you want to accompany the forwarded email

6 Tap on the **Send** button

Deleting Email

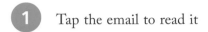

You can delete email a couple of different ways

1 Tap the email to read it

2 When finished, tap the trash icon at the bottom of the screen

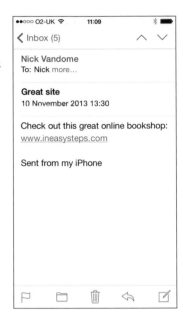

Alternative method

1 In the email list view slide your finger across the email from right to left (do not open it)

2 A red **Trash** box should appear

3 Tap **Trash** and the email will be deleted

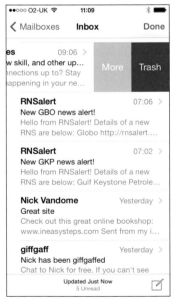

Yet another way of deleting email is

1 Go to **Inbox** and tap the **Edit** button at the top right

2 The contents of the inbox are displayed in Edit mode

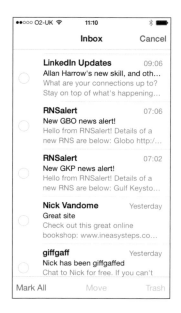

3 Tap each email you want to delete and a blue circle will appear in the left column

4 Hit **Trash** when you are ready to delete

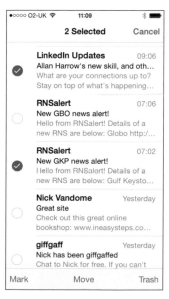

Move Email to Folders

If you have an IMAP account, such as an iCloud account, you can see your folders on the server. You can move mail from your Inbox to another folder. This helps keep your mail organized, and your Inbox uncluttered.

1 Open the email you want to move and tap on the **Folder** button on the bottom toolbar

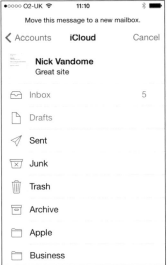

2 Tap on the folder into which you want to move the email

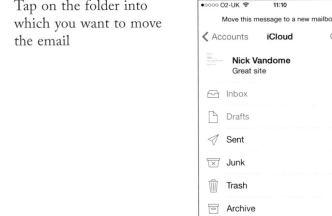

3 The email appears in the selected folder

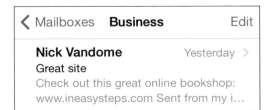

9 Accessibility Settings

The iPhone is well suited for people with visual or motor issues. This chapter details the Accessibility options on the iPhone, so that everyone can get the most out of it.

Accessibility Settings

Many people with visual impairments should be able to make use of devices like the iPhone. With the standard default configuration they may run into problems, but the iPhone has many settings that can be modified to make them more usable.

What features are available?

- VoiceOver

- Zoom

- White on Black

- Mono Audio

- Speak Auto-text

Most of these features will work with most applications, apart from VoiceOver which will only work with the iPhone's standard (pre-installed) applications.

1 Tap on the **Settings** app

2 Tap on the **General** tab

3 Tap on the **Accessibility** link

4 The **Accessibility** options are displayed – tap on a link to access more options

5 Or, drag the button **On** or **Off** to access these

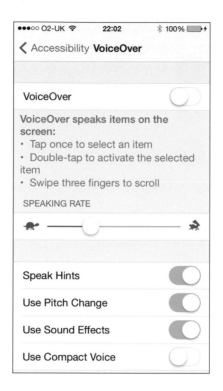

6 Swipe up and down the page to view the full range of options for each item

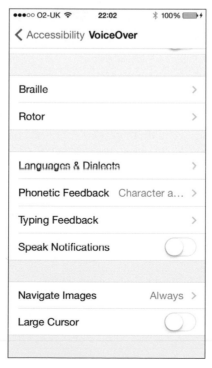

Activate Settings on iPhone

Switching on VoiceOver

1 Go to **Settings > General > Accessibility**

2 Activate **VoiceOver** as shown below

3 When finished, you may wish to switch it off again

Tap on VoiceOver and drag the button on to activate it

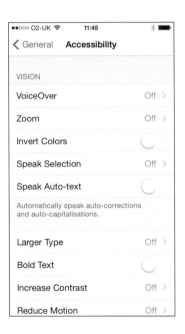
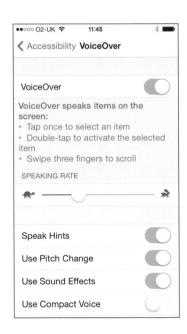

Switch to Zoom to enlarge (Zoom cannot be used with VoiceOver)

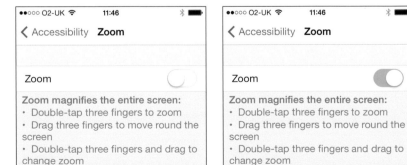

Other accessibility settings

1 Go to **Settings** > **General** > **Accessibility**

2 Activate **Invert Colors**

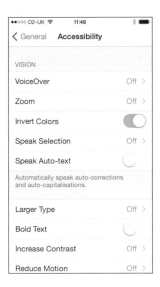

3 Activate **Zoom** to increase the size of the items on the screen (see page 183)

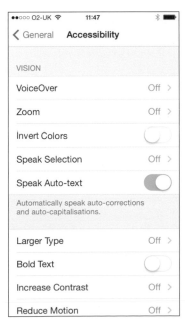

VoiceOver

VoiceOver
This speaks what's on the screen, so you can tell what's on the screen even if you cannot see it. It describes items on the screen and, if text is selected, VoiceOver will read the text.

Speaking rate
This can be adjusted using the settings.

Typing feedback
VoiceOver can provide this: go to **Settings > General > Accessibility > VoiceOver > Typing Feedback**.

Languages
VoiceOver is available in languages other than English (but is not available in all languages).

VoiceOver Gestures
When VoiceOver is active, the standard touchscreen gestures operate differently:

Tap	Speak item
Flick right or left	Select next or previous item
Flick up or down	Depends on Rotor Control setting
Two-finger tap	Stop speaking current item
Two-finger flick up	Read all from top of screen
Two-finger flick down	Read all from current position
Three-finger flick up or down	Scroll one page at a time
Three-finger flick right or left	Go to next or previous page
Three-finger tap	Speak the scroll status

Apple Support for VoiceOver
See: *h*ttp://support.apple.com/kb/HT3598

Zoom

The iPhone touchscreen lets you zoom in and out of elements on the screen. Zoom will let you magnify the whole screen, irrespective of which application you are running.

Turn Zoom on and off

1 Go to **Settings > General > Accessibility > Zoom**

2 Tap the Zoom **Off/On** switch

3 You cannot use Zoom and VoiceOver at the same time

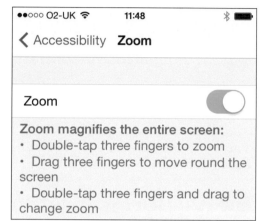

Zoom in and out

1 Double tap the screen with three fingers

2 The screen will then magnify by 200%

Increase magnification

1 Use **three fingers** and drag to the top of the screen (increase magnification) or bottom (decrease magnification).

2 Move around the screen

3 Drag or flick the screen with three fingers

Other Accessibility Settings

Increase Contrast

This feature enhances the contrast on the iPhone, which may make it easier for some people to read.

Activate Increase Contrast

1 Go to **Settings > General > Accessibility**

2 Tap the **Increase Contrast** link

3 Drag the **Increase Contrast** button to **On**

Mono Audio

This combines the sound of both left and right channels into a mono audio signal played through both sides.

Turn Mono Audio on and off

1 Go to **Settings > General > Accessibility**

2 Switch on **Mono Audio**

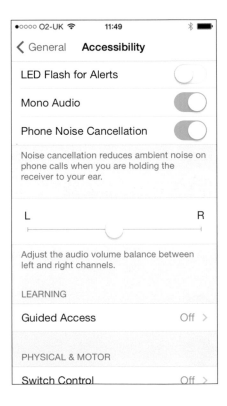

Speak Auto-text

This setting enables the iPhone to speak text corrections and suggestions as you type text into the iPhone.

Turn Speak Auto-text on

1 Go to **Settings > General > Accessibility**

2 Switch on **Speak Auto-text**

3 Speak Auto-text works with VoiceOver and Zoom

Closed Captioning

This needs to be turned on in the Accessibility Settings:

1 Go to **Settings > General > Accessibility > Subtitles & Captioning**

2 Slide **Closed Captions** button to **On** to activate

Large phone keypad

The keypad of the iPhone is large, making it easy for people who are visually impaired to see the digits.

1 Tap the **Phone** icon (on the dock)

2 Tap the **keypad** icon (4th icon from left)

Hot tip

Closed Captioning adds subtitles to video content. Not all videos contain Closed Captioning information but where it is available you can access it by turning on Closed Captions.

Restrictions

If children are going to be using your iPhone, or if they have their own, you may want to restrict the type of content they can access:

1 Tap on the **Settings** app

2 Tap on the **General** tab

General

3 Tap on the **Restrictions** link

Restrictions   Off >

4 By default the restrictions are disabled, i.e. grayed-out so they cannot be accessed. Tap on the **Enable Restrictions** button

⟨ General   **Restrictions**

Enable Restrictions

ALLOW:

Safari

5 Set a passcode in order to set restrictions

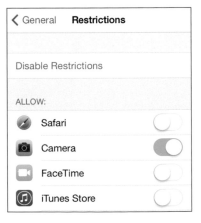

Set Passcode   Cancel

Enter a Restrictions Passcode

● ● ● —

6 For the items you want to restrict, drag their buttons to **Off**. These icons will no longer appear on the iPhone's Home screen

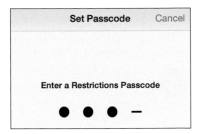

⟨ General   **Restrictions**

Disable Restrictions

ALLOW:

Safari

Camera

FaceTime

iTunes Store

Beware

If you are restricting items for someone, make sure that you discuss it with them and explain your reasons for doing this, rather than just letting them find out for themselves when they try to use an app.

10 Working with Apps

There are thousands of apps for the iPhone, catering for every conceivable need. This chapter looks at how to find apps, install them, and remove them. It also takes you through some of the apps in each category, to give you an idea of the range of apps available for the iPhone, both paid-for and free.

Organizing Apps

When you start downloading apps you will probably soon find that you have dozens, if not hundreds, of them. You can move between screens to view all of your apps by swiping left or right with one finger.

To move an app between screens, tap and hold on it until it starts to jiggle and a cross appears in the corner. Then drag it to the side of the screen. If there is space on the next screen the app will be moved here.

As more apps are added it can become hard to find the apps you want, particularly if you have to swipe between several screens. However, it is possible to organize apps into individual folders to make using them more manageable.

To do this:

1   Press on an app until it starts to jiggle and a blue cross appears at the top-left corner

2   Drag the app over another one

3 A folder is created, containing the two apps. The folder is given a default name, usually based on the category of the apps

4 Tap on the folder name and type a new name if required

Beware

Only top-level folders can be created, i.e. sub-folders cannot be created. Also, one folder cannot be placed within another.

5 Click on the **Done** button on the keyboard or the **Home** button to finish creating the folder

6 Click the **Home** button again to return to the Home screen (this is done whenever you want to return to the Home screen from an apps folder)

7 The folder is added on the Home screen. Tap on this to access the items within it

Hot tip

If you want to rename an apps folder after it has been created, tap and hold on it until it starts to jiggle. Then tap on it and edit the folder name as in Step 5.

About the App Store

While the built-in apps that come with the iPhone are flexible and versatile, it really comes into its own when you connect to the App Store. This is an online resource and there are thousands of apps there that can be downloaded and then used on your iPhone, including categories from Lifestyle to Travel and Medical.

To use the App Store, you must first have an Apple ID. This can be obtained when you first connect to the App Store. Once you have an Apple ID you can start exploring the App Store:

1 Tap on the **App Store** app on the Home screen

2 The latest available apps are displayed on the Homepage of the App Store, including the Editor's Choice, featured in the top panel

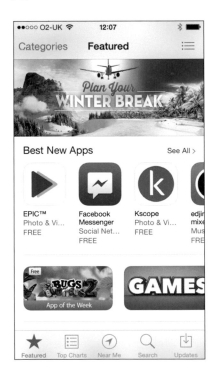

3 Tap on these buttons to view the apps according to **Featured**, **Top Charts**, **Near Me** and **Updates**

Try downloading a free app to get started such as our **In Easy Steps** app. Type in easy steps in the Search box. You'll see:

Tap the app and follow the instructions to install the app.

Viewing apps

To view apps in the App Store and read about their content and functionality:

1 Tap once on an app

2 General details about the app are displayed

3 Swipe left or right here to view additional information about the app and view details

4 **Reviews** and **Related** apps are available from the relevant buttons, next to the **Details** button

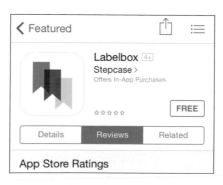

Finding Apps

Featured

Within the App Store, apps are separated into categories according to type. This enables you to find apps according to particular subjects. To do this:

1 Tap on the **Featured** button on the toolbar at the bottom of the App Store

2 Scroll left and right to view different category headings

Tap on the **Categories** button to view apps in specific categories.

3 Scroll up the page to view additional categories and **Quick Links**

Top Charts

To find the top rating apps:

1   Tap on the **Top Charts** button on the toolbar at the bottom of the App Store

2   The top overall paid for, free and top grossing apps are displayed

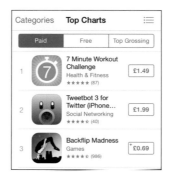

3   To find the top apps in different categories, tap on this button

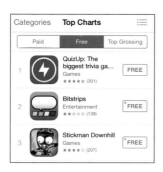

Beware

There are now so many apps, it may be difficult to find what you want. Try using the search tool and enter a word or words that describe what you are looking for.

4   Tap on the **Categories** button    Categories

5   The top apps for that category are displayed

Beware

Do not limit yourself to just viewing the top apps. Although these are the most popular, there are also a lot of excellent apps within each category.

...cont'd

Near Me

This is a feature which suggests appropriate apps according to your current geographic location. To use this:

1. Tap on the **Near Me** button on the toolbar at the bottom of the App Store

2. Tap on the **Show Popular Apps Near Me** link

Near Me shows apps that are popular near your current location.

Show Popular Apps Near Me

Depending on your location, there may not be any apps featured in the **Near Me** section.

3. Tap on the **OK** button to enable the App Store to use your location (**Location Services** must be activated for this to work)

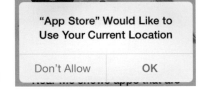

"App Store" Would Like to Use Your Current Location

Don't Allow   OK

4. Recommendations will appear in the **Popular Near Me** window, based on your location

...cont'd

Searching for apps

Another way to find apps is with the App Store Search box, which is located at the top-right corner of the App Store window. To use this:

1 Tap in the **Search** box to bring up the iPhone virtual keyboard

2 Enter a search keyword or phrase

3 Suggested apps appear as you are typing

4 Tap on an app to view it

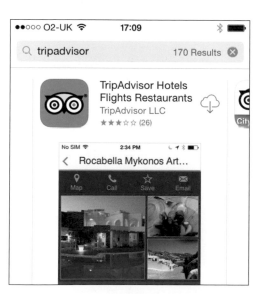

Installation Process

To install apps from the App Store:

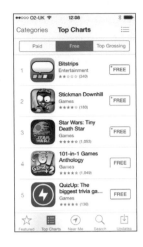

1 Find the app you want using **App Store** on the iPhone

2 Tap the **Price** or **Free** tab

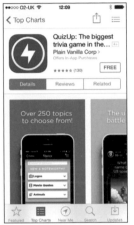

Don't forget

You need to remember your iTunes account password – you will be asked for this each time you try to install or update an app, even if it is free.

3 Tap on the **Install** button

4 Enter your iTunes password

5 The app will install

Updating Apps

The publishers of apps provide updates which bring new features and improvements. You don't have to check your apps to see if there are updates – you can set them to be updated automatically through the Settings app. To do this:

1 Open **Settings** and tap on the **iTunes & App Store** link

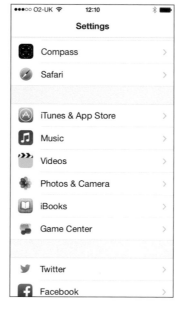

2 Drag the **Updates** button to **On** to enable automatic updates for apps

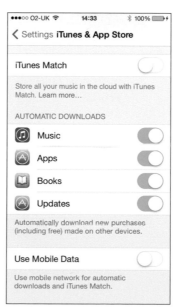

If your App Store icon has a red circle with a number inside, it means there's an update for one or more of your apps. If updates are not set to automatic, the apps can be updated manually in the **Updates** section of the App Store.

Removing Apps

To remove apps from your iPhone:

1 **Press and hold** the app you want to remove

2 All the apps on the screen will start jiggling and you will see an **x** at the top of the app

Don't forget

If you remove an app, it can be reinstalled from the App Store. The app will have a cloud icon next to it and will be free to reinstall, even if it was a paid-for app.

3 Tap the **x** and the app will be deleted

4 Tap on the **Delete** button to confirm your action

Games

Angry Birds Space HD
Rovio Entertainment Ltd
★★★★☆ (15)

Fruit Ninja
Halfbrick Studios
★★★★⯪ (343)

Bad Piggies
Rovio Entertainment Ltd
★★★★⯪ (73)

Plague Inc.
Ndemic Creations
★★★★⯪ (365)

TETRIS®
Electronic Arts
★★★☆☆ (21)

Cut the Rope
Chillingo Ltd
★★★★⯪ (246)

Angry Gran Run
AceViral.com
★★★★⯪ (832)

Entertainment

Keep Calm and Carry On
Back Bay Bytes LLC

Based on the old World War II posters you can create you own versions using this app.

Sports Car Engines
ARE Apps Ltd

Brings you the noises and sounds of some of the most powerful and icon cars in the world.

Action Movie FX
Bad Robot Interactive
★★★★☆ (30)

Add Hollywood effects to videos you create using your iPhone (or iPad).

Gyroscope
acrossair
★★★★☆ (6)

This is an educational app since it emulates 3-D gyroscopes and is very realistic.

Utilities

Battery Magic
myNewApps.com
★★★★☆ (129)

Battery utilities are big business, and there are loads of them on the App Store. This one makes a nice sound when you have reached full charge and has a large battery display.

DIY List
Hurryforward Ltd
★★★★☆ (5)

Builders, home DIY enthusiasts, interior decorators and others should find this list-maker and to-do app useful.

MyCalendar Mobile
K-Factor Media, LLC.
★★★★★ (9)

Import birthdays from Facebook, message friends with customizable messages.

Safe Note
Bedroom Developers Ltd
★★★★½ (166)

This app lets you keep notes, lists and reminders away from prying eyes by letting you password protect them.

Social Networking

LinkedIn
LinkedIn Corporation
★★★★☆ (117)

Popular social networking site for PC and Mac and now available on iOS devices. Useful for headhunters and those wishing to find work.

The two most popular social networking sites, **Facebook** and **Twitter**, also have apps that can be downloaded from the App store.

Status Shuffle for Facebook
Social Graph Studios
★★⯪☆☆ (17)

This app updates your Facebook status using random updates. Not sure why this is useful but seems popular.

Skype for iPhone
Skype Communications S.a.r.l
★★☆☆☆ (52)

The ubiquitous Skype has now found a home on the iPhone with this great Skype app.

WhatsApp Messenger
WhatsApp Inc.

★★★★☆ (1,371)

This is a cross-platform smartphone messenger (iPhone, Android, BlackBerry and Nokia) which lets you message your friends and receive push notifications.

Music

GarageBand
Apple
★★★★☆ (482)

Great app on the Mac to write and produce music and now available for the iPhone in all its glory.

Piano Chord Key
Matt Whitehead

As the title suggests, this app shows you what piano keys to hit when you want to generate chords. It helps with chord progressions, too.

TuneIn Radio Pro
TuneIn
★★★★⯪ (79)

A radio app, lets you stream music using AirPlay.

TuneIn Radio
TuneIn
★★★★☆ (74)

With this app you can listen to, and record, more than 40,000 AM/FM radio stations.

Productivity

Evernote
Evernote
★★★★☆ (100)

This is an amazing piece of software for the Mac and PC and now it's available on the iPhone. Because of the iPhone's small screen it is trickier to use than the computer equivalents.

Dropbox
Dropbox
★★★☆☆ (105)

Now you can access your Dropbox files directly from your iPhone. If you don't have this for your computer – get it now!

Numbers
Apple
★★⯨☆☆ (58)

Numbers is part of the iWork suite on the Mac. Useful spreadsheet with great chart options. Saves data to iCloud.

GoodReader for iPhone
Good.iWare Ltd.
★★★★☆ (11)

This is one of the available PDF readers for the iPhone. Does a nice job, and has a clear interface.

Lifestyle

eBay
eBay Inc.
★★★★½ (666)

Most of us use eBay but using a browser to check your auctions on the iPhone is not great. This app solves all those problems.

Momento (Diary/Journal)
d3i Ltd
★★★★★ (5)

Diary app lets you capture moments through the day, tag memorable events, etc.

Jamie's 20 Minute Meals
Zolmo
★★½☆☆ (70)

Jamie Oliver seems to be everywhere so why not on the iPhone? The app has loads of his best recipes and cooking tips.

My Secret Folder™
Red Knight Interactive
★★★★☆ (541)

Store private photos and videos. Looks like a folder but is actually an app. If someone tries to break into the app it takes a picture and will even email you if there is a break-in attempt which helps to recover stolen iPhones.

Reference

WolframAlpha
Wolfram Group LLC
★★★★⯪ (9)

Heavyweight reference tool for physics, chemistry, earth sciences and much more.

Brian Cox's Wonders of the Universe
HarperCollins Publishers Ltd
★★★★⯪ (22)

Astronomy app based on Brian Cox's TV program. Explore the universe using this app. Highly rated!

Google Search
Google, Inc.
★★★⯪☆ (110)

The popular search app that also provides a range of other services. However, it does take you to a browser to use the actual applications themselves. Still very useful.

Dictionary!!
Farlex, Inc.
★★★★⯪ (68)

This has definitions of more than 200,000 words. It also has an advanced spellchecker and a thesaurus.

Travel

London Tube Deluxe
Malcolm Barclay
★★★☆☆ (16)

There are several Tube map apps out there but this one does it even better. It has journey planner, departure boards, and is multilingual.

Google Earth
Google, Inc.
★★☆☆☆ (597)

This remains an amazing application on the computer and the iPhone version is superb too. (It is now included in the Google Maps app.)

Flightradar24 Pro
Flightradar24 AB
★★★★☆ (57)

Air traffic radar, see airplane traffic and more.

Live Train Times - Real-time UK Train Departur...
Anecdote Software
★★★★☆ (12)

Provides train times for UK trains. Similar apps are available for other locations.

Sports

SkyDroid - Golf GPS
Goldstein Technologies LLC
★★★★★ (20)

For golf enthusiasts. Track distance of your drives, find the distance to any point on course and many other features.

ESPN Goals
ESPN
★★★☆☆ (10)

Provides live scores for UK, European and International footballs teams.

Sky Sports for iPhone
BSkyB
★★★★☆ (9)

Live video content and interviews. However, to use the app you will need a Sky Mobile TV subscription.

Fantasy Premier League 2013/14
Premier League
★★☆☆☆ (13)

Has more than 2.5 million players. Pick your teams and play in this fantasy football game.

Navigation

MobiMaps with Google Maps and Street View
Brainflash
★★★★⯪ (17)

Uses built-in iPhone maps. Provides street view (this view is not included with the iPhone's Maps app).

Waze Social GPS, Maps & Traffic
Waze Inc.
★★★★⯪ (806)

A Wiki app where drivers add data constantly making it very up-to-date in terms of traffic, accidents, diversions, etc. A great satnav and free!

Light - LED Flashlight
Jason Ting
★★★★★ (1,052)

Another app which makes your iPhone light up like a torch. Helpful when you're in a dark place and have forgotten to bring a torch with you.

ATM Locator - Find the Nearest ATMs
Ombros Brands Inc.
★☆☆☆☆ (6)

Rather than wander for miles looking for a hole in the wall, this app will tell you where the nearest ATM is located.

Health & Fitness

Get Ripped – Fat Burner & Muscle Toning
fitivity inc

The ultimate app for getting the ripped look you always dreamed of. Provides great photos of the exercises, diet and sleep advice and loads more.

Full Fitness : Exercise Workout Trainer
Mehrdad Mehrain
★ ★ ★ ★ ⯨ (193)

Another work-out app for those seeking the body-beautiful. Useful information in terms of workouts aimed at all levels from beginner to the seasoned pro.

Sleep Cycle alarm clock
Northcube AB
★ ★ ★ ★ ⯨ (222)

Monitors your movements during sleep and tells you how good your sleep cycle is. Wakes you up at the optimum time.

Carbs & Cals - Count your Carbs & Calories…
Chello Publishing

This app helps you work out what to eat and what not to eat.

News

Zite
Zite, Inc.
★★★★⯪ (148)

Beautiful magazine app with personalized interface. You can share stories with Facebook, Twitter, and Instapaper.

The Economist on iPhone (UK)
The Economist
★★☆☆☆ (23)

Get the Economist news stories on your iPhone. Provides the Editor's selection and must-read articles.

Instapaper
Instapaper, LLC
★★★★☆ (14)

Cool app for saving long web pages and blogs so you can read them offline later. There are numerous user settings such as fonts, size, and others to help make the content more readable for you.

Flipboard: Your Social News Magazine
Flipboard Inc.
★★★★★ (191)

Similar to Zite, a customized reader, with sharing for Facebook, Twitter, and Instapaper.

Photography

Camera+
tap tap tap
★★★⯪☆ (33)

Improve your shots, high quality zoom, cropping and other tools.

Camera All In One
jun shen
★★⯪☆☆ (5)

There are loads of camera apps for the iPhone but this one seems to be several apps in one, providing color effects, zoom, antishake, geotagging and time-stamping. Very useful.

iPhoto
Apple
★★★☆☆ (115)

iPhoto has been popular for years on the Mac and this iPhone version has loads of great features.

iMovie
Apple
★★★★⯪ (300)

iMovie on the Mac makes movie editing easy and the same is true of Apple's iPhone version.

Finance

Debt Manager
MH Riley Ltd
★★★★⯨ (186)

Get your debts under control, create plans to help you pay off your debts.

Spending Log
Corbenic Consulting
★★★★★ (8)

Track your expenditure, works out where you can cut back in order to save money.

PayPal
PayPal, an eBay Company
★★☆☆☆ (44)

PayPal is the preferred method of payment for eBay and many websites now and it's great to have PayPal as a separate app on the iPhone.

MoneyBook - finance with flair
noidentity gmbh

Great for personal finance, and has a companion web app. You can export your transactions as emails and the app will help you with your budgeting.

Business

Documents To Go®
Standard - Office Suite
DataViz, Inc.

If you ever need to edit Microsoft Office files on the iPhone this app will make the task easy. You can sync files from your desktop to your iPhone once you download the mini DTG app for Mac or PC.

Mail+ for Outlook
iKonic Apps LLC
★★☆☆☆ (14)

An alternative mail client to the inbuilt Mail. Read, write, and reply to Outlook email.

Dragon Dictation
Nuance Communications
★★★☆☆ (91)

Rather than type your emails and text why not dictate and let Dragon do the transcription? Easy to use.

JotNot Scanner
MobiTech 3000 LLC

Multipage document scanner. Saves files as PDF, PNG, JPEG and allows emailing of documents.

Education

Tiny Garden
Milo Creative

Helps children learn new words as they play. You can record your own words and several languages are available.

Quick Math for Kids
Phuong Tran Hoai

Basic math educational tool. Includes times tables.

Design and Technology
J Plimmer

Now a regular school subject, the D&T app helps kids get more out of their studies. The app includes quizzes and other features to help with learning in a fun way.

Star Walk™ - 5 Stars Astronomy Guide
Vito Technology Inc.
★★★★⯨ (40)

This is your personal planetarium providing all you need to know about the cosmos, with a ton of features that make astronomy even more interesting.

Weather

WeatherPro
MeteoGroup Deutschland...
★★★★☆ (73)

Seven-day forecasting, wind direction, wind speed, sharing of data on Facebook and Twitter.

Awesome Live Weather Clock
mobsub

Covers more than 25,000 cities. Automatic location detector.

Weather Live Free
Apalon Apps
★★★★☆ (129)

Another weather app with features similar to the others. Provides freeze alerts.

Ski Club Snow Reports
Sotic Ltd
★★☆☆☆ (161)

Covers 250 ski resorts, snow depths, piste conditions, and live weather with web cams. For those who love to ski this has to be one app you can't live without.

Books

Apple's ebook app, as featured on the iPad, is also on the iPhone. You can browse, buy, read and store ebooks and PDFs for reading anywhere you want. Tons of user settings to make the reading even easier.

Kindle
AMZN Mobile LLC
★ ★ ★ ★ ☆ (95)

This app is the gateway to Kindle books which you can buy and read just as you would with iBooks. There's a huge selection of books to choose from.

QI Lite for iPhone
Faber and Faber

Based on the popular quiz program.

Marvel Comics
Marvel Entertainment

Features all your favorites such as Iron Man, Captain America and others. You can also back up your books using the website.

Medical

Pregnancy +
Health & Parenting Ltd
★★★★⯪ (137)

Daily information on your pregnancy. Health, diet and exercise. Weight tracker, birth planning, etc.

ECG Guide
QxMD Medical Software

Largest ECG library on iPhone. ECG interpreter, 100 MCQs.

Blood Pressure Companion
Maxwell Software

Add and edit blood pressure readings. Export your data in CSV, HTML and PDF formats.

Learn Muscles : Anatomy Quiz & Refer...
Real Bodywork
★★★★★ (28)

Beautiful reference and educational tool. Quizmaker and great graphics.

11 Solving Problems

The iPhone occasionally misbehaves – an app will not close, or the iPhone may malfunction. This section looks at how to fix common problems and provides some helpful websites. The chapter also helps you find your lost or stolen iPhone.

General iPhone Care

The iPhone is a fairly robust gadget but, like any complex piece of electronic hardware, it may suffer from knocks, scratches, getting wet and other problems.

Cleaning the body and screen

The touchscreen is supposed to be scratch resistant. In fact, there are YouTube videos showing people trying to scratch the screen by placing the iPhone into a plastic bag containing keys and shaking the whole thing around. Amazingly, the screen seems not to scratch. Then they put it in a blender and it, well, got blended. So it's definitely not blender-proof!

The best way to clean an iPhone is with a lint-free cloth such as the one above used for cleaning reading glasses. Make sure there is no grit or sand on the body or screen and gently rub with the cleaning cloth. This should bring back the shine without scratching the glass or the back of the phone.

Occasionally the screen may get very greasy and a little soap helps to get the grease off

1 Put a few drops of dishwashing liquid in warm water

2 Get some paper kitchen towel and dip this into the water

3 Wring out the kitchen towel so it is not dripping wet and lightly wipe over the screen and rest of the casing

4 Dry off using a clean cloth

Keep iPhone Up-to-Date

Apple releases updates to the iPhone operating system periodically.

Is your iPhone fully up-to-date?

1 Tap on the **Settings** app

2 Tap on the **General** tab (if there is a number after it, this indicates that there is an update)

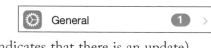

3 Tap on the **Software Update** link to view the current status of your operating system

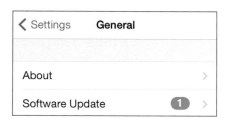

4 If there is an update available it will be displayed

5 Tap on the **Install Now** button

Software updates for iPhone users are provided free by Apple. If one becomes available, download and install it.

Maximize iPhone Battery

The iPhone is a bit of a power hog. Browsing the web, listening to music and watching videos drains power. If you only make a few phone calls each day, your iPhone will last a couple of days between charges. But most people use it for far more than this and their battery will last about a day.

Tweaks to ensure maximum battery life

1 Switch Off **Wi-Fi** if you don't need it

2 Switch Off **Bluetooth** if you don't need it

3 Switch On **Battery Percentage** indicator, under **Settings > General > Usage**

4 Switch off **3G** if you don't need this, under **Settings > Mobile**

5 Collect your **email manually**, under **Mail, Contacts, Calendars > Fetch New Data**

6 Set **Auto-lock** to a short period, e.g. 1 minute, under **Settings > General > Auto-Lock**

7 Always hit the **Off** button when you have finished using the iPhone (screen goes black which uses less power)

8 Reduce the brightness of your screen, under **Settings > Wallpapers & Brightness**

9 Consider using **Airplane mode** for maximum conservation of power!

Hot tip

You can conserve battery power by switching off Wi-Fi and Bluetooth. Instead of opting for push email, you can check for email manually.

Beware

If you use Airplane mode you will not receive any calls, texts or notifications.

Manage Storage	>
BATTERY USAGE	
Battery Percentage	⬤
TIME SINCE LAST FULL CHARGE	
Usage	0 Minutes
Standby	0 Minutes

< Settings **Wallpapers & Brightness**

BRIGHTNESS

☀ ———————— ☀

Auto-Brightness ⬤

Restart, Force Quit and Reset

Restart the iPhone

If the iPhone misbehaves, or applications act strangely, you can restart the iPhone.

1 **Hold down** the Sleep/Wake button

2 When you see the **Slide to Power Off** appear, **swipe this to the right**

3 Leave the iPhone for a couple of minutes then press the **Sleep/Wake** button again and let the phone restart

Quit an app

Sometimes apps misbehave and you want to quit them and reopen. To do this, press the Home button twice to access the multitasking window.

Swipe left or right to find the app that you want to quit and swipe it up to the top of the screen.

Force Quit the iPhone

1 Press the **Sleep/Wake** and the **Home button** at the same time

2 The screen will suddenly turn black and the iPhone will automatically restart

...cont'd

Resetting the iPhone

There are various aspects of your iPhone that can be reset to their factory defaults. These include resetting the Home Screen Layout, Network Settings and the Keyboard Dictionary. You can also reset all of the settings on the iPhone, or the Content and Settings. This erases all of the content and resets the iPhone to its factory, unused, condition. You may want to do this if you have been using the iPhone and then want to give it to someone else. To do this:

1 Select **Settings > General** and tap on the **Reset** button (at the bottom of the page)

2 All of the Reset options are displayed. Tap on the **Erase All Content and Settings** button

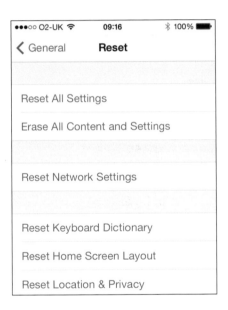

3 Enter a passcode if you use one to lock your iPhone

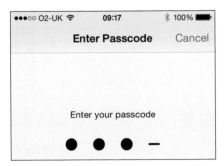

4 Tap on the **Erase iPhone** button

This will delete all media and data, and reset all settings.

Erase iPhone

Cancel

5 Since it is a serious action you will be asked if you are sure. Tap on the **Erase iPhone** button again

Are you sure you want to continue? All media, data and settings will be erased. This cannot be undone.

Erase iPhone

Cancel

6 Enter your Apple ID and tap on the **Erase** button to return your iPhone to its factory condition

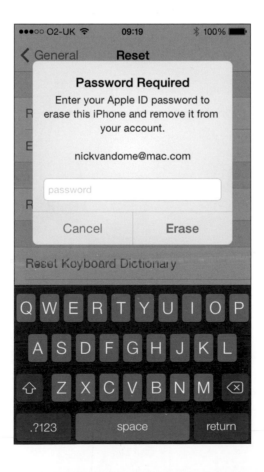

●●●○○ O2-UK 🛜   09:19   ✳ 100% ▇

❮ General   **Reset**

Password Required
Enter your Apple ID password to erase this iPhone and remove it from your account.

nickvandome@mac.com

| password |

Cancel   Erase

Reset Keyboard Dictionary

Q W E R T Y U I O P
A S D F G H J K L
⇧ Z X C V B N M ⌫
.?123   space   return

Hot tip

If you reset the contents and settings for your iPhone you can restore them when you next turn on the phone. This can be done from an iCloud or an iTunes backup and is done at the **Set Up iPhone** step of the setup process.

225

Apple Resources

Visit Apple!

The first place you should look for help is the Apple site. After all, iPhone is their creation so they should know more than anyone.

The iPhone and iPhone Support areas are packed with information, tutorials and videos.

Useful URLs

http://www.apple.com/iphone/

http://www.apple.com/support/iphone/

The first place to look for hints, tips and fixes is Apple's website, which is chock full of information and videos.

Technology Experts

David Pogue's Top 10 iPhone tips...
on the O'Reilly site are worth reading (David Pogue is always
worth reading – he loves technology and loves all things Apple).

Useful URLs
**http://broadcast.oreilly.com/2009/07/david-pogues-top-10-
tips-for-t.html**

David's New York Times blog is fantastic, and you can find it here
http://pogue.blogs.nytimes.com/

Visit the iLounge!

iLounge has long provided loads of hints and tips for iPods. These guys review hardware, accessories and provide reviews of new gear for the iPod, the iPhone and the iPad.

What does the site offer?

1 News

2 Reviews of apps and accessories

3 Forums

4 Software

5 Help

6 Articles

Other Useful Websites

I Use This

Provides reviews of iPhone apps, and lets you know how many people are actually using the apps.

What's on iPhone

Largely a review site but it also provides information about hardware and for people interested in developing for the iPhone.

If You Lose Your iPhone

Maybe you were out late and dropped your iPhone but can't quite remember where? Or perhaps it's in the house but you are not 100% sure. If you use iCloud to look for the location of your iPhone it may help you recover the iPhone. Certainly, if it's at home you will soon know, because the map location will show you where the iPhone is. The iPhone does actually have to be on, and transmitting to the cellular network, in order for Find My iPhone to work.

Find My iPhone also allows you to erase the entire contents of your iPhone remotely. This means that if it gets stolen, you can remotely erase the iPhone and prevent whoever stole your iPhone from getting their hands on your personal data.

Set up Find My iPhone
Before you use Find My iPhone it has to be set up on the phone itself. To do this:

Hot tip

If for no other reason, it is worth getting an iCloud account so you can track your iPhone and erase the contents if it gets stolen.

1 Tap on the **Settings** app

2 Tap on the **iCloud** tab

3 If the **Find My iPhone** functionality is Off, drag the button to **On**

4 Tap on the **OK** button in the Find My iPhone dialog box to activate this functionality

Find My iPhone

This enables Find My iPhone features, including the ability to show the location of this iPhone on a map.

Cancel   OK

...cont'd

Locating your iPhone

Once you have set up Find My iPhone you can then use the
online service to locate it, lock it, or erase its contents.

1 **Log in to iCloud** (**www.icloud.com**)

2 Click on the
**Find My
iPhone**
button

3 To use the Find My iPhone
functionality you have to sign
in again with your Apple ID

4 The
location
of your
iPhone
is shown
on a map

...cont'd

5 Click on the **i** symbol to see options for your lost iPhone

6 Details about the phone, and options for what you can do, are displayed

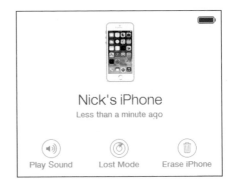

7 Click on the **Play Sound** button to send an alert sound to the phone. A message is displayed to let you know that a sound has been sent to your iPhone

8 Click on the **Lost Mode** button to lock your iPhone remotely. You have to enter a passcode to do this and this will be required to unlock the iPhone

9 Click on the **Erase iPhone > Erase** button if you are worried that someone might compromise the data on your iPhone

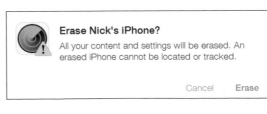

Index

T

U